The Imitation of Christ

THOMAS À KEMPIS

BARBOUR
PUBLISHING

© 2013 by Barbour Publishing, Inc.

Editorial assistance by Jill Jones.

Print ISBN 978-1-62029-767-4

eBook Editions:
Adobe Digital Edition (.epub) 978-1-62416-072-1
Kindle and MobiPocket Edition (.prc) 978-1-62416-071-4

Cover images: Shutterstock

Published by Barbour Publishing, Inc., P.O. Box 719, Uhrichsville, Ohio 44683, www.barbourbooks.com

Our mission is to publish and distribute inspirational products offering exceptional value and biblical encouragement to the masses.

ecpa Member of the
Evangelical Christian
Publishers Association

Printed in the United States of America.

CONTENTS

1. Of the Imitation of Christ and Contempt for the World / 2. Of Thinking Humbly of Oneself / 3. Of the Knowledge of Truth / 4. Of Prudence in Action / 5. Of the Reading of Holy Scriptures / 6. Of Lustful Thoughts / 7. Of Fleeing from Meaningless Hope and Pride / 8. Of the Danger of Too Much Familiarity / 9. Of Obedience and Subjection / 10. Of the Danger of an Overabundance of Words / 11. Of Seeking Peace of Mind and Spiritual Progress / 12. Of the Uses of Adversity / 13. Of Resisting Temptation / 14. Of Avoiding Rash Judgment / 15. Of Works of Charity / 16. Of Bearing with the Faults of Others / 17. Of the Resolutions of a Religious Person / 18. Of the Love of Solitude and Silence / 19. Of Contrition of Heart / 20. Of the Contemplation of Human Misery / 21. Of Meditation on Death / 22. Of the Judgment and Punishment of the Wicked / 23. Of the Zealous Improvement of Our Whole Life

INTRODUCTION

For more than five hundred years, *The Imitation of Christ* has been one of the world's most widely read books of Christian devotions. Many editions have appeared in various languages since the first printed version appeared in 1472, shortly after the introduction of Johannes Gutenberg's moveable type.

For seventy years, from early manhood until the day of his death at age ninety-two, Thomas à Kempis dedicated himself to acts of devotion. He was a writer of letters, hymns, and biographies, and is said to have copied the Bible four times.

The Imitation of Christ has as its foundation biblical texts—more than a thousand of them—grouped together under general headings: the spiritual life, inward things, and internal consolation. Nearly every book of the Bible is represented here, though this devotional classic draws chiefly from the Psalms, the Gospels, and the Epistles.

The book that follows is an abridged, lightly updated version of Thomas à Kempis's classic. Read slowly, in brief portions at a time, it can encourage a new commitment to the Lord Jesus Christ.

BOOK I
ADMONITIONS PROFITABLE FOR THE SPIRITUAL LIFE

———◆◆◆———

CHAPTER 1
OF THE IMITATION OF CHRIST AND CONTEMPT FOR THE WORLD

"He who follows Me shall not walk in darkness," says the Lord (John 8:12). These are the words of Christ, and they teach us how far we must imitate His life and character if we desire true illumination and deliverance from all blindness of heart. Let it be our most earnest study, therefore, to dwell on the life of Jesus Christ.

His teaching surpasses all teaching of holy men, and those who have His Spirit find in it "the hidden manna" (Revelation 2:17). But there are many who, though they frequently hear the gospel, feel little longing for it, because they do not have the mind of Christ. He, therefore, who desires to fully and with true wisdom understand the words of Christ should strive to conform his whole life to the mind of Christ.

It is not deep words that make a man holy and upright; it is a good life that makes a man dear to God. I would rather feel contrition than be skillful in the definition of it. If you know the whole Bible and the sayings of all the philosophers, what good will it do you without the love and grace of God? All is meaningless, except to love God and serve only Him. That is the highest wisdom, to cast the world behind us and to reach forward to the heavenly kingdom.

It is meaningless, then, to seek after and trust in the riches that will perish. It is meaningless, too, to covet honors and to lift up ourselves on high. It is meaningless to follow the desires of the flesh and be led by them, for this will bring misery in the end. It is meaningless to desire a long life and to have little care for a good life. It is meaningless to take thought only for the life that now is and not to look forward to the things that will be hereafter. It is meaningless to love what quickly passes away and not to hurry to where eternal joy abides.

Think often of the saying, "The eye is not satisfied with seeing, nor the ear filled with hearing" (Ecclesiastes 1:8). Strive, therefore, to turn away your heart from love of the things that are seen and to set it on the things that are not seen. For those who follow after their own fleshly lusts defile the conscience and destroy the grace of God.

CHAPTER 2

OF THINKING
HUMBLY OF ONESELF

What profit is knowledge without the fear of God? Better is a lowly peasant who serves God than a proud philosopher who watches the stars and neglects the knowledge of himself. He who knows himself well is vile in his own sight, neither does he regard the praises of men. If I knew all the things that are in the world and were not walking in love, how would it help me before God, who is to judge me according to my deeds?

Rest from excessive desire for knowledge, for therein is found much distraction and deceit. Those who have knowledge desire to appear learned and to be called wise. There are many things to know that provide little or no profit to the soul. And foolish is he who focuses on things other than those that contribute to his soul's health. Many words do not satisfy the soul, but a good life refreshes the mind, and a pure conscience gives great confidence.

The greater and more complete your knowledge, the more severely will you be judged, unless you have lived righteously. Therefore do not be prideful about any skill or knowledge that you have. If it seems to you that you know many things and understand them well, know also that there are many more things that you do not know. Why do you desire to lift yourself above another, when there are many more knowledgeable and more skilled in the scriptures than you? If you want to know and learn anything beneficial, love to be unknown and to be counted as nothing.

The best and most profitable lesson is when a man truly knows and judges himself humbly. To think humbly of one's self and to think always kindly and highly of others, this is great and perfect wisdom. Even if you see your neighbour sin openly or grievously, you ought not to consider yourself better than he, for you know not how long you will keep your integrity. All of us are weak and frail; consider no man more frail than yourself.

Chapter 3

Of the Knowledge of Truth

The more simplicity a man has within himself, the more things and the deeper things he understands, and that without hard work, because he receives the light of understanding from above. The spirit that is pure, sincere, and steadfast is not distracted though it has much work to do, because it does all things for the honor of God and strives to be free from all thoughts of self-seeking. A person who is good and devout determines beforehand within his own heart the work he has to do, and so is not drawn away by the desires of his selfish will but subjects everything to the judgment of right reason. Who has a harder battle to fight than he who strives for self-mastery? This should be our endeavor: to master self and thus daily grow stronger than self and strive for perfection.

All perfection has some imperfection joined to it in this life. A lowly knowledge of yourself is a surer way to God than the deep searchings of man's learning. Not that learning is to be avoided nor the taking account of anything that is good; but a good conscience and a holy life is better than all. And because many seek knowledge rather than good living, they go astray and bear little or no fruit.

How many perish through empty learning in this world who care little for serving God. And because they love to be great more than to be humble, they have become "futile in their thoughts" (Romans 1:21). He only is truly great who has great love. He is truly great who considers himself small. He is the truly wise man who considers all earthly things as garbage that he may gain Christ. And he is the truly learned man who does the will of God and forsakes his own will.

Chapter 4

Of Prudence in Action

We must not trust every word of others or every feeling within ourselves, but must cautiously and patiently try each matter, whether it is of God. Sadly, we are so weak that we find it easier to believe and speak evil of others than good. But those who are perfect do not believe every word of gossip, for they know man's weakness, that it is prone to evil.

This is great wisdom: to not be hasty in action or stubborn in our own opinions. A part of this wisdom also is not to believe every word we hear, nor to tell others all that we hear, even though we believe it. Take counsel with a man who is wise and has a good conscience, and seek to be instructed by one better than yourself, rather than to follow your own ideas. A good life makes a man wise in God's eyes and gives him experience in many things. The more humble a man is in himself, and the more obedient toward God, the wiser will he be in all things, and the more will his soul be at peace.

Chapter 5

Of the Reading of Holy Scriptures

It is truth we must look for in Scripture, not cunning words. All Scripture ought to be read in the spirit in which it was written. We ought to read books that are devotional and simple, as well as those that are deep and difficult. And let not the education of the writer be a stumbling block to you, whether he has little or much learning, but let the love for the pure truth draw you to read. Ask not who has said this or that, but focus on what he says.

Men pass away, but the truth of the Lord endures forever. God speaks to us in different ways. If you want to profit from your reading, read humbly, simply, and honestly.

Chapter 6

Of Lustful Thoughts

Whenever a man desires something he does not have, he immediately becomes restless. The proud and greedy are never at rest, while the poor and humble of heart abide in peace. The person who is not yet wholly dead to self is easily tempted and overcome by small matters. It is hard for the one who is weak in spirit and still partly carnal and inclined to the pleasures of the senses to withdraw himself altogether from earthly desires. And therefore, when he withdraws himself from these, he is often sad and easily angered if anyone opposes his will.

But if, on the other hand, he yields to his desire, immediately he is weighed down by the condemnation of his conscience, for he has followed his own desire and yet in no way attained the peace he hoped for. For true peace of heart is to be found in resisting temptation, not in yielding to it. Therefore there is no peace in the heart of a person who is carnal, but only in one who is fervent toward God and living the life of the Spirit.

CHAPTER 7

OF FLEEING FROM MEANINGLESS HOPE AND PRIDE

Meaningless is the life of anyone who puts their trust in men or any created thing. Do not be ashamed to be the servant of others for the love of Jesus Christ, and to be considered poor in this life. Build your hope in God. Do what lies in your power, and God will help your good intent. Trust not in your learning, nor in the cleverness of anyone, but rather trust in the favor of God, who resists the proud and gives grace to the humble.

Boast not in your riches if you have them, nor in your friends if they are powerful, but in God, who gives all things, and in addition to all things desires to give Himself. Do not be proud because of your strength or beauty of body, for with only a slight sickness it will fail and wither away. Do not be vain about your talents or abilities, lest you displease God, from whom comes every good gift.

Do not consider yourself better than others, or you may appear worse in the sight of God, who knows what is in man. Do not be proud of your good works, for God's judgments are different than the judgments of man, and what pleases man is often displeasing to Him. If you have any good, believe that others have more, and so you may preserve your humility. It is not harmful to you if you place yourself below all others; but it is very harmful if you place yourself above even one. Peace is ever with the humble person, but in the heart of the proud there is envy and anger.

CHAPTER 8

OF THE DANGER OF
TOO MUCH FAMILIARITY

Do not open your heart to every person but to one who is wise and fears God. Do not be a flatterer of the rich, nor willingly seek the company of the great. Let your company be the humble and the simple, the devout and the gentle, and let your conversation be edifying.

Chapter 9

Of Obedience and Subjection

It is a great thing to live in obedience, to be under authority, and not to be at our own disposal. Far safer is it to live in subjection than in a place of authority. Many are obedient out of necessity rather than love. They will not gain freedom of spirit unless with all their heart they submit themselves for the love of God. Though you run here and there, you will not find peace unless you are in humble submission to the authority of those who are set over you.

Every man willingly follows his own bent and is more inclined toward those who agree with him. But if Christ is among us, then it is necessary that we sometimes yield up our own opinion for the sake of peace. Who is so wise as to have perfect knowledge of all things? Therefore do not trust your own opinion too much, but be ready also to hear the opinions of others. Though your own opinion is good, yet if for the love of God you forego it and follow someone else's, you will benefit.

I have often heard that it is safer to receive counsel than to give it. Each opinion may be good, but to refuse to listen to others when reason or occasion requires it is a mark of pride or willfulness.

CHAPTER 10

OF THE DANGER OF AN OVERABUNDANCE OF WORDS

Why do we gossip so continually, seeing that in so doing we rarely avoid harming our conscience? We like talking so much because we hope by our conversations to gain some comfort, and because we seek to refresh our wearied spirits by a variety of thoughts. And we very willingly talk and think of those things that we love or desire, as well as those we most dislike.

But it often serves no purpose, for this outward consolation is a hindrance to the inner comfort that comes from God. Therefore must we watch and pray. If it is right and desirable for you to speak, speak things that edify. Devout conversation on spiritual things helps our spiritual progress.

CHAPTER 11

OF SEEKING PEACE OF MIND AND SPIRITUAL PROGRESS

We may enjoy abundance of peace if we refrain from busying ourselves with the words and doings of others, and things that do not concern us. How can a man enjoy peace for long when he occupies himself with other men's matters, and meanwhile pays little heed to himself?

We are too occupied with our own affections and too anxious about earthly things. Seldom, too, do we entirely conquer even a single fault, nor are we zealous for daily growth in grace. And so we remain lukewarm and unspiritual.

If we were fully watchful of ourselves and not bound in spirit to outward things, then we might be wise for salvation and make progress in divine contemplation. Our great stumbling block is that, not being freed from our affections and desires, we do not strive to enter into the perfect way. And when even a little trouble strikes, too quickly are we discouraged and run to the world to give us comfort.

If we want to strive to stand firm in the battle, then we should see the Lord helping us from heaven. For He Himself is always ready to help those who strive and who trust in Him; indeed, He provides for us opportunities to strive in order that we may win the victory.

If each year saw one fault rooted out of us, we would move quickly toward perfection. But on the contrary, we often feel that we were better and holier when we were first converted than after many years of salvation. Zeal and progress ought to increase day by day, yet now it seems a great thing if one is able to retain some portion of his first fervor. If we would put some slight stress on ourselves at the beginning, then later we would be able to do all things with ease and joy.

It is a hard thing to break through a habit, and a yet harder thing to go contrary to our own will. Yet if you do not overcome easy obstacles, how will you overcome harder ones? Resist your will at the beginning and unlearn a bad habit, or it may lead you little by little into worse difficulties. Oh, if you knew what peace your holy life would bring you and what joy to others, I think you would be more zealous for spiritual growth.

CHAPTER 12

OF THE USES OF ADVERSITY

It is good for us that we sometimes have sorrows and adversities, for they often help us remember that we are only strangers on this earth and to not put our trust in any worldly thing. It is good that we sometimes endure oppositions and are unfairly judged when we do and mean what is good. For these things help us to be humble and seek more earnestly the witness of God.

Therefore ought a person to rest wholly on God so that he need not seek much comfort from others. When a man who fears God is afflicted or tried or oppressed, then he sees that he needs God all the more, since without God he can do no good thing.

CHAPTER 13

OF RESISTING TEMPTATION

As long as we live in the world, we cannot be without trouble and trial. No man is so perfect in holiness that he never has temptations, nor can we ever be wholly free from them.

Yet temptations are for our good, even though they are hard to bear; for through them we are humbled, purified, instructed. All saints have passed through much tribulation and temptation and have experienced the benefits. And those who did not endure temptation fell away.

There is no person wholly free from temptations as long as he lives, because we have the root of temptation within ourselves. One temptation or sorrow passes, and another comes, and we will always have something to suffer, for we have fallen from perfect happiness. Many who seek to flee from temptations fall yet more deeply into them. By flight alone we cannot overcome, but by endurance and true humility we are made stronger than all our enemies.

He who resists only outwardly and does not pull sin up by the root will get nowhere; rather temptations will return to him the more quickly and will be the more terrible. Little by little, through patience and longsuffering, you will conquer with the help of God. In the midst of temptation seek counsel often, and do not deal harshly with one who is tempted, but comfort and strengthen him.

The beginning of all temptations is instability of temper and lack of trust in God. For even as a ship without a helm is tossed about by the waves, so is a man who is careless and lacking in purpose tempted. As fire tests iron, so does temptation the upright man. Often we know not what strength we have, but temptation reveals to us what we are. Nevertheless, we must watch, especially when we are first tempted, for that is when the enemy is most easily mastered, when he is not allowed to enter the mind but is met outside the door as soon as he has knocked. For first the simple suggestion comes to the mind, then the strong imagination, afterwards pleasure and assent. And so little by little the enemy enters in altogether, because he was not resisted at the beginning. And the longer a person delays his resistance, the weaker he grows, and the stronger grows the enemy against him.

Some people suffer their most grievous temptations in the beginning of their conversion, some at the end. Some are sorely tried their whole life long. Some are tempted only lightly, according to the wisdom and justice of God, who knows the character and circumstances of men and orders all things for the welfare of His children.

Therefore we should not despair when we are tempted but should cry all the more fervently to God that He will help us and that He will, as Paul said, "with the temptation. . .make the way of escape, that [we] may be able to bear it" (1 Corinthians 10:13). Let us therefore humble ourselves under the mighty hand of God in all temptation and trouble, for He will save and exalt those who are humble.

In temptations and troubles a man is proved, as far as what progress he has made, and in that his reward is the greater and his virtue appears all the more. Nor is it a great thing if a man is devout and zealous as long as he suffers no affliction; but if he behaves himself patiently in the time of adversity, then is there hope of great progress. Some are kept safe from great temptations but are overtaken in little ones, that the humiliation may teach them not to trust themselves.

CHAPTER 14

OF AVOIDING RASH JUDGMENT

Beware that you not judge others. In judging others a man often falls easily into sin; but in judging and examining himself he always labors for a good purpose. So often do we judge a matter according to how it strikes our fancy, for we easily fall short of true judgment because of our own personal feelings. If God were always the sole object of our desire, we would be less easily troubled by our erring judgment.

But often some secret thought lurking within us, or even some outward circumstance, turns us aside. Many are secretly seeking their own ends in what they do, yet know it not. They seem to live in good peace of mind as long as things go well with them, but if their desires are frustrated, they are immediately displeased.

No man is very easily led to see through the eyes of another. If you rest more on your own reason or experience than on the power of Jesus Christ, your light will come slowly, for God wills us to be perfectly subject to Himself and our reason to be exalted by abundant love toward Him.

CHAPTER 15

OF WORKS OF CHARITY

Without love no work is beneficial, but whatever is done in love brings forth good fruit; for God considers what a man is able to do more than the greatness of what he does.

He does much who loves much. He does much who does well. He does well who ministers to the public good rather than his own. Often what seems to be love is actually carnality, because it springs from natural inclination, self-will, hope of repayment, desire of gain.

He who has true and perfect love does not seek his own good but desires that God alone be glorified. He envies no one, because he does not long for selfish joy, nor does he rejoice in himself but longs to be blessed in God as the highest good. He credits good to no one but God.

Chapter 16

Of Bearing with the Faults of Others

Those things that a man cannot improve in himself or in others he ought to bear patiently, until God will otherwise ordain. Nevertheless you ought, when you find such faults, to ask God to sustain you, that you might be able to bear them with a good will.

If one who is once or twice admonished refuses to listen, do not strive with him, but commit all to God, that His will may be done and His honor be shown in His servants, for He knows well how to convert the sinful to good. Try to be patient in bearing with other men's faults and weaknesses, for you yourself also have many things that have to be put up with by others. If you cannot make your own self what you desire, how will you be able to fashion another to your liking? We are ready to see others made perfect, and yet we do not fix our own shortcomings.

We want others to be corrected, but we do not want to be corrected ourselves. The freedom of others displeases us, but we are dissatisfied that our own wishes are denied us. We desire rules to be made that restrain others, but by no means will we allow ourselves to be restrained. Thus therefore does it plainly appear how seldom we weigh our neighbor in the same balance as we weigh ourselves. If all men were perfect, what then should we have to suffer from others for God?

But God has thus ordained that we may learn to bear one another's burdens, because no one is without defect; but we must learn to bear with one another, to comfort one another, to help, instruct, admonish one another. How much strength each man has is best proven by adversity.

CHAPTER 17

OF THE RESOLUTIONS OF A RELIGIOUS PERSON

The life of a Christian ought to be adorned with all virtues, that he may be on the inside what he appears to be on the outside. And it should be even better on the inside than on the outside, for God is a discerner of our hearts. We ought to kindle our hearts to zeal, as if each day were the first day of our conversion, and to say, "Help me, O God, in my good resolutions, and in Your holy service, and grant that this day I may make a good beginning, for up until now I have done nothing!"

According to our resolution so is the rate of our progress, and much diligence is needed for those who want to make good progress. For if he who resolves bravely often falls short, how will it be for him who resolves rarely or feebly? The resolution of the righteous depends more on the grace of God than on their own wisdom, for in Him they always put their trust.

CHAPTER 18

OF THE LOVE OF
SOLITUDE AND SILENCE

Seek a suitable time for your meditation, and think frequently of the mercies of God toward you. Study such matters as bring you sorrow for sin rather than amusement.

It is easier to be completely silent than it is to not speak too much. He, therefore, who seeks to reach that which is hidden and spiritual must spend time with Jesus in solitude. No man safely talks but he who loves to be quiet. No man safely rules but he who loves to submit. No man safely commands but he who loves to obey.

No man safely rejoices but he who has a good conscience. But the boldness of wicked men springs from pride and presumption.

Often those who stand highest in the esteem of men fall the more grievously because of their overconfidence. Therefore it is very profitable to many that they should be frequently assaulted with inner temptation so they do not become overconfident and prideful, or else lean too heavily on the consolations of the world. Oh, how good a conscience would that man keep who never sought a joy that passes away, who never became entangled with the world! How great a peace would he possess if he cast off all worldly cares and thought only of divine things and built his whole hope on God!

No man is worthy of heavenly consolation but he who has diligently exercised himself in holy contrition. If you want to feel contrition within your heart, enter into your chamber and shut out the world, as it is written, "Meditate within your heart on your bed, and be still" (Psalm 4:4). In solitude you will find what you often lose when you are with people. Solitude, if you continue in it, grows sweet, but if you do not continue in it, it wearies you. If you dwell in it, it will afterwards be to you a dear friend and a most pleasant solace.

In quiet the devout soul learns the hidden things of the scriptures. Therein it finds a fountain of tears in which to wash and cleanse itself each night, that it may grow the more dear to its Maker as it grows further from all worldly distraction. To him who withdraws himself from his friends God will draw near. It is better to be unknown and watch oneself than to neglect oneself and work wonders.

Why would you want to see what you may

not have? "The world is passing away, and the lust of it" (1 John 2:17). The desires of sensuality take you out and about, but when an hour is past, what do you bring home but a weight on your conscience and distraction of heart? A frivolous going forth often ends in a sorrowful return, and a passionate evening makes a sad morning. So does all carnal joy begin pleasantly, but in the end it destroys.

What can you see anywhere that can continue long under the sun? You believe, perhaps, that you will be satisfied, but you will never find satisfaction. If you could see all things in front of you at once, what would it be but a meaningless vision? Lift up your eyes to God on high, and pray that your sins may be forgiven. Leave meaningless things to vain men, and mind the things God has commanded you. Shut your door behind you and call Jesus your beloved. Remain with Him, for you will not find so great a peace anywhere else. If you had not listened to meaningless talk, you would have better kept yourself in good peace. But because it sometimes delights you to hear new things, you must therefore suffer trouble of heart.

CHAPTER 19

OF CONTRITION OF HEART

If you want to make any progress, keep yourself in the fear of God, and do not long to be too free, but restrain all your senses under discipline and do not give yourself up to senseless mirth. Give yourself to contrition of heart and you will find devotion. Contrition opens the way for many good things that dissipation usually quickly loses.

Through lightness of heart and neglect of our shortcomings we feel not the sorrows of our soul, but often vainly laugh when we have good cause to weep. There is no true liberty nor real joy except in the fear of God with a good conscience. Happy is he who can cast away every cause of distraction and bring himself to the one purpose of holy contrition. Happy is he who casts away from him whatever may stain or burden his conscience.

Do not busy yourself with the affairs of others, nor entangle yourself with the business of great people. Always keep your eyes on yourself first of all, and give advice to yourself before you give it to all your dearest friends. If you do not have the favor of people, do not be discouraged, but let your concern be that you not think too highly of yourself.

Often it is from poverty of spirit that the wretched body is so easily led to complain. Pray therefore humbly to the Lord that He will give you the spirit of contrition, and say in the language of the prophet, "Feed me, O Lord, with the bread of tears, and give me tears to drink in great measure" (see Psalm 80:5).

CHAPTER 20

OF THE CONTEMPLATION OF HUMAN MISERY

You are miserable wherever you are and wherever you turn, unless you turn to God. Why are you upset when something does not happen according to your wishes and desires? Who has everything according to their will? There is no man in the world free from trouble or anguish. Who is he who has the happiest lot? Even he who is strong to suffer for God.

There are many foolish and unstable men who say, "See what a prosperous life that man has, how rich and how great he is, how powerful, how exalted." But lift up your eyes to the good things of heaven, and you will see that all these worldly things are nothing, they are utterly uncertain, indeed, they are wearisome, because they are never possessed without care and fear. The happiness of man lies not in the abundance of temporal things, but a moderate portion is sufficient for him. The more a man desires to be spiritual, the more distasteful does the present life become to him.

Do not lose your desire for progress toward

spiritual things. Arise, begin this very moment, and say, "Now is the time to do; now is the time to fight." When you are troubled, then you are nearest to blessing. You must go through fire and water that God may bring you into a wealthier place. Unless you put force upon yourself, you will not conquer your faults. As long as we carry about with us this frail body, we cannot be without sin, we cannot live without weariness and trouble. Gladly would we have rest from all misery; but because through sin we have lost innocence, we have lost all true happiness. Therefore must we be patient and wait for the mercy of God.

CHAPTER 21

OF MEDITATION ON DEATH

What good does it do to live long when we improve so little? Long life does not always improve a person but often increases guilt all the more. Oh, that we might spend a single day in this world as it ought to be spent! Many there are who count the years since they were converted, and yet often how little is the fruit in their lives. If it is a fearful thing to die, it may be a more fearful thing to live long.

Happy and wise is he who strives to be in life what he wants to be found in death! For a perfect contempt of the world, a fervent desire to excel in virtue, the love of discipline, the painfulness of repentance, readiness to obey, denial of self, submission to any adversity for love of Christ: these are the things that will give great hope of a happy death. While you are healthy you have many opportunities to do good works; but when you are sick, I know not how much you will be able to do.

CHAPTER 22

OF THE JUDGMENT AND PUNISHMENT OF THE WICKED

In all that you do, remember the end and how you will stand before a strict judge, from whom nothing is hid, who is not bribed with gifts, nor accepts excuses, but will judge righteous judgment. O foolish sinner, what will you answer to God, who knows all your sins? Why do you not provide for yourself against the day of judgment, when no one will be able to be excused or defended by another, but each will bear his burden alone? Now does your labor bring forth fruit, now is your weeping acceptable, your groaning heard, your sorrow well pleasing to God and cleansing to your soul.

Even here on earth the patient man finds many opportunities to purify his soul: when hurt or offended he grieves more for the other's malice than for his own wrong; when he prays heartily for those who are spiteful toward him and forgives them from his heart; when he is not slow to ask pardon from others; when he is swifter to compassion than to anger; when he frequently denies himself and strives to subdue the flesh to the spirit. Better is it now to purify the soul from sin than to cling to sins from which we must be purged hereafter. Truly we deceive ourselves by the inordinate love we have for the flesh.

The more you follow the flesh, the more heavy will your punishment be.

There is no sin that will not be visited with its own appropriate punishment. The proud will be filled with utter confusion, and the covetous will be pinched with miserable poverty. An hour's pain there will be more grievous than a hundred years here of the bitterest penitence. No quiet will be there, no comfort for the lost, though here sometimes there is respite from pain and enjoyment of the solace of friends. Be sorrowful for your sins now so that in the day of judgment you may have boldness with the blessed. He who now submits himself in humility to the judgments of men will stand up to judge. The poor and humble man will have great confidence, while the proud is overcome by fear on every side.

Then will it be seen that he who learned to be a fool and despised for Christ was the wise man in this world. Then will all tribulation patiently borne delight us, while the mouth of the ungodly will be stopped. Then will every godly man rejoice, and every profane man will mourn.

Then the humble garment will become beautiful, and the precious robe will be considered vile. Then the poor cottage will be more commended than the gilded palace. Then enduring patience will have more might than all the power of the world. Then simple obedience shall be more highly exalted than all worldly wisdom.

Then a good conscience will rejoice more than learned philosophy. Then contempt of riches will have more weight than all the treasure of the children of this world. Then will you find more comfort in having prayed devoutly than in having lived sumptuously. Then holy deeds will be far stronger than many fine words. Then a strict life and sincere penitence will bring deeper pleasure than all earthly delight.

CHAPTER 23

OF THE ZEALOUS IMPROVEMENT OF OUR WHOLE LIFE

Be watchful and diligent in God's service and remember often why you have renounced the world. Was it not that you might live for God and become a spiritual person? Be zealous therefore for your spiritual profit, for you will soon receive the reward of your labors, and neither fear nor sorrow will come near you any longer. If you remain faithful and zealous in labor, doubt not that God will be faithful and generous in rewarding you. It is your duty to have a good hope that you will attain the victory, but you must not feel too secure lest you become slothful or proud.

"Trust in the Lord, and do good; dwell in the land, and feed on His faithfulness" (Psalm 37:3). One thing holds many back from progress: the dread of difficulty, or the labor of the conflict. Nevertheless, those who strive bravely to conquer their faults advance further than others in virtue, for a person profits most and gains greater grace in the areas where he most overcomes himself and mortifies himself in spirit.

But not everyone has the same passion to conquer and mortify, yet he who is diligent will attain more virtue, although he has stronger passion than another who has a more temperate disposition but is less fervent in the pursuit of virtue. Two things especially prevail in helping us improve in holiness: firmness to withdraw ourselves from the sin to which by nature we are most inclined, and earnest zeal for the good we are most lacking. And earnestly strive also to guard against and subdue those faults that displease you most in others.

Gather some profit to your soul wherever you are, and wherever you see or hear good examples, stir yourself to follow them, but where you see anything that is wrong, be careful that you not do the same; or if at any time you have done it, strive quickly to amend yourself. As your eyes observe others, so also are the eyes of others on you. How sweet and pleasant is it to see zealous, godly, disciplined, temperate people; and how sad is it to see them undisciplined, not practicing the duties to which they are called. How hurtful a thing it is to neglect the purpose of their calling and turn to things that are none of their business.

Be mindful of the duties you have undertaken, and set always before you the remembrance of the Crucified. Truly ought you to be ashamed as you look on the life of Jesus Christ, because you have not yet endeavored to conform yourself more to Him, though you have been in the way of God a long time. A religious man who exercises himself seriously and devoutly in the most holy life and passion of our Lord will find there abundantly all things that are profitable and necessary for him, and there is no need to seek anything better beyond Jesus. Oh! If Jesus crucified would come into our hearts, how quickly and completely would we learn all that we need to know!

He who is earnest receives and bears well all things that are laid on him. He who is careless and lukewarm has many troubles and suffers anguish on every side. He who is living without discipline is exposed to grievous ruin. He who seeks easier and lighter discipline will always be in distress, because one thing or another will give him displeasure.

When a man has come to the place where he seeks comfort from no created thing, then does he begin to perfectly enjoy God and is well contented with whatever happens to him. Then will he neither rejoice for much nor be sorrowful for little, but he commits himself completely and with full trust to God, who is all in all to him.

Always remember your end and how the time that is lost does not return. Without care and diligence you will never develop virtue. If you begin to grow cold, things will begin to go poorly for you, but if you give yourself to zeal you will find much peace and will find your labor lighter because of the grace of God and the love of virtue. A zealous and diligent man is ready for all things. It is greater labor to resist sins and passions than to toil in bodily labors. He who does not shun small faults falls little by little into greater. In the evening you will always be glad if you spent the day profitably. Watch over yourself, stir yourself up, admonish yourself, and however things are with others, do not neglect yourself. The more violence you do to yourself, the more progress you will make. Amen.

Book II
Admonitions Concerning the Inner Life

Chapter 1
Of the Inward Life

"The kingdom of God is within you" (Luke 17:21), says the Lord. Turn with all your heart to the Lord and forsake this miserable world, and you will find rest for your soul. Learn to despise outward things and to devote yourself to spiritual things, and you will see the kingdom of God come within you. For the kingdom of God is peace and joy in the Holy Spirit, and it is not given to the wicked. All His glory and beauty is from within, and there it pleases Him to dwell. He often visits the inward man and holds with him sweet conversation, giving him soothing consolation, much peace, wonderful friendship.

Prepare your heart for this bridegroom that He may come to you and dwell within you, for He says, "If anyones loves Me, he will keep My word; and My Father will love him, and We will come to him and make Our home with him" (John 14:23). Give place to Christ, therefore, and refuse entrance to all others. When you have Christ, you are rich and have everything you need. He will be your provider and faithful watchman in all things, so that you have no need to trust in people, for people soon change and swiftly pass away, but Christ remains forever and stands by us firmly to the end.

Put your complete trust in God and let Him be your fear and your love. He will answer for you Himself and will do for you what is best. You will never have rest unless you are closely united to Christ within you.

Why do you focus on the things of this earth, since this is not the place of your rest? In heaven should your habitation be, and all earthly things should be looked on as if they are passing by. All things pass away and you with them. Be careful that you not cling to them or you will be taken with them and perish. Let your contemplation be on the Most High, and let your prayers be directed to Christ without ceasing. If you cannot behold heavenly things, rest in the passion of Christ. For if you devoutly fly to the wounds of Jesus, you will find great comfort in tribulation, nor will the slights of men trouble you much, and you will easily bear their unkind words.

Christ also, when He was in the world, was despised and rejected of men, and in His greatest need was left by His friends to bear these reproaches. Christ was willing to suffer and be despised, and dare you complain about any hardship? Christ had adversaries and people who opposed Him, and do you wish to have all men be your friends? How will your patience gain its crown if no adversity troubles you? If you are unwilling to suffer any adversity, how will you be the friend of Christ? Sustain yourself with Christ and for Christ if you desire to reign with Christ.

If you had once entered into the mind of Jesus and had tasted even a little of His tender love, then you would care nothing for your own convenience or inconvenience, but would rather rejoice at the trouble brought upon you, because the love of Jesus makes a man despise himself. He who loves Jesus and is inwardly true and free from passions and lust is able to turn himself readily to God and to rise above himself in spirit and enjoy fruitful peace.

If all were well with you and you were purified from sin, all things would work together for your good. For this cause do many things often trouble you, because you are not yet perfectly dead to yourself nor separated from all earthly things. Nothing so defiles and entangles the heart of man as impure love toward created things. If you reject outward comfort, you will be able to contemplate heavenly things and be joyful inwardly.

Chapter 2

Of Lowly Submission

Do not keep track of who is for you or against you, but take care that God is with you in whatever you do. Have a good conscience and God will defend you, for he whom God helps no man's perverseness will be able to hurt. If you know how to hold your peace and suffer, without doubt you will see the help of the Lord. He knows the time and the way to deliver you, therefore must you surrender yourself to Him. It is God's place to help and deliver from all confusion. Often it is very profitable for keeping us in greater humility when others know and rebuke our faults.

When a man humbles himself for his faults, he then easily pacifies others and quickly satisfies those who are angry with him. God protects and delivers the humble man, He loves and comforts the humble man, to the humble man He inclines Himself, on the humble He bestows great grace, and when he is discouraged He raises him to glory. To the humble He reveals His secrets and sweetly draws and invites him to Himself. The humble man, having received reproach, is enjoying sufficient peace, because he rests on God and not on the world. Reckon not yourself to have profited in any way unless you feel yourself to be inferior to all.

Chapter 3

Of the Good, Peaceable Person

First keep yourself in peace, and then will you be able to be a peacemaker toward others. A peaceable person does more good than a knowledgeable person. A good, peaceable person converts all things into good. He who dwells in peace is suspicious of none, but he who is discontented and restless is tossed about with many suspicions and is neither quiet himself nor allows others to be quiet. He often says what he ought not to say, and omits what was expedient for him to do. He focuses on others' duties and neglects those to which he is bound himself. Therefore be zealous over yourself first, and then you may be righteously zealous concerning your neighbor.

You know well how to excuse and color your own deeds, but you will not accept the excuses of others. It would be more just to accuse yourself and excuse your brother. If you want others to bear with you, you must bear with others. It is no great thing to mingle with the good and the meek, for this is naturally pleasing to all, and every one of us willingly enjoys peace and likes best those who think like us. But to be able to live peaceably with the difficult and perverse, the disorderly, or those who oppose us, this is a great grace and a thing to be commended.

CHAPTER 4

OF A PURE MIND
AND SIMPLE INTENTION

By two wings is a person lifted above earthly things: simplicity and purity. Simplicity ought to be in the intention, purity in the affection. Simplicity reaches toward God, purity takes hold of Him. No good action will be distasteful to you if you are free within from passions and lust. If you reach after and seek nothing but the will of God and the benefit of your neighbor, you will entirely enjoy inward liberty.

If you were good and pure within, then would you look upon all things without being hurt and understand them rightly. A pure heart sees the very depths of heaven and hell. As each one is inwardly, so judges he outwardly. If there is any joy in the world, surely the man of pure heart possesses it, and if there is tribulation and anguish anywhere, the defiled conscience knows it best. As iron cast into the fire loses its rust and is made to glow, so the man who turns himself completely over to God is freed from slothfulness and changed into a new man.

When a man begins to grow lukewarm, then

he fears a little labor and willingly accepts outward consolation; but when he begins to perfectly conquer himself and to walk courageously in the way of God, then he counts as nothing those things that used to seem so grievous to him.

CHAPTER 5

OF SELF-ESTEEM

The spiritually minded man puts care of himself before all cares, and he who diligently attends to himself easily keeps silence concerning others. You will never be spiritually minded and godly unless you are silent concerning other men's matters and pay careful attention to yourself.

You will make great progress if you keep yourself free from all temporal care. Let nothing be great, nothing high, nothing pleasing, nothing acceptable to you except God Himself and the things of God. The soul that loves God looks not to anything that is beneath God. God alone is eternal and incomprehensible, filling all things, the solace of the soul, and the true joy of the heart.

CHAPTER 6

OF THE JOY OF A
GOOD CONSCIENCE

A good conscience is the glory of a good man. Have a good conscience and you will ever have joy. A good conscience is able to bear much and is joyful in the midst of adversities; an unclean conscience is ever fearful and disturbed. You will rest sweetly if your heart does not condemn you. The wicked never have true joy and never feel peace, for " 'there is no peace,' says my God, 'for the wicked' " (Isaiah 57:21).

To glory in tribulation is not grievous to him who loves, for such glorying is glorying in the cross of Christ. Brief is the glory that is given and received of men. Sadness always goes hand in hand with the glory of the world. The joy of the upright is from God and in God, and their joy is in the truth. He who cares for neither praises nor reproaches has great tranquility of heart.

He whose conscience is pure will easily be contented and filled with peace. You are none the holier if you are praised, nor the more unrighteous if you are reproached. You are what you are, and you cannot be better than God pronounces you to be. If you consider well what you are inwardly, you will not care what men say to you. "Man looks at the outward appearance, but the Lord looks at the heart" (1 Samuel 16:7). It is the sign of a humble spirit to always do well and to think little of oneself.

CHAPTER 7

OF LOVING JESUS ABOVE ALL THINGS

Blessed is he who understands what it is to love Jesus and to despise himself for Jesus' sake. He must give up all that he loves for his Beloved, for Jesus will be loved alone above all things. The love of created things is deceiving and unstable, but the love of Jesus is faithful and lasting. He who clings to created things will fall with their slipperiness; but he who embraces Jesus will stand upright forever. Love Him and hold Him as your friend, for He will not forsake you when all depart from you.

Cling to Jesus in life and death, and commit yourself to His faithfulness, who alone is able to help you when all men fail you. Your Beloved is such, by nature, that He will put up with no rival but desires to possess your heart alone. If you learn to put away from you every earthly thing, Jesus will freely take up His abode with you.

Chapter 8

Of the Intimate Love of Jesus

When Jesus is present all is well and nothing seems hard, but when Jesus is not present everything is hard. When Jesus does not speak within, any comfort is worthless, but if Jesus speaks but a single word, great is the comfort we experience. Happy is the hour when Jesus calls you from tears to the joy of the spirit!

What can the world profit you without Jesus? To be without Jesus is the deepest hell, and to be with Jesus is sweet paradise. If Jesus is with you no enemy can hurt you. He who finds Jesus finds a good treasure, indeed, good above all good; and he who loses Jesus loses much, indeed, more than the whole world.

It takes great skill to know how to live with Jesus, and to know how to stay close to Jesus is great wisdom. Be humble and peaceable and Jesus will be with you. Be godly and quiet, and Jesus will remain with you. You can quickly drive Jesus away and lose His favor when you turn away to earthly things. And if you have sent Him away, to whom will you flee and whom then will you seek for a friend? Without a friend you cannot live long, and if Jesus is not your friend above all, you will be very sad and desolate. It is preferable to have the whole world against you than to have Jesus offended with you.

You ought to bring a bare, clean heart to God if you desire to be ready to see how gracious the Lord is. When the grace of God comes to a man, then he becomes able to do all things, and when it departs he is poor and weak and overcome by troubles. In these you are not to be cast down nor to despair, but to rest with calm mind on the will of God and to bear all things that come upon you to the praise of Jesus Christ.

CHAPTER 9

OF THE LACK OF ALL COMFORT

It is not too hard to despise human comfort when divine comfort is present. It is a great thing to be able to bear the loss of both human and divine comfort, and for the love of God to willingly bear exile of heart and in nothing seek oneself. What great matter is it if you are cheerful and devout when favor comes to you? Pleasantly enough does he ride whom the grace of God carries. And what marvel is it if he who is carried by the Almighty feels no burden?

Mightily must a person strive within himself before he learns to overcome himself and to draw his whole heart toward God. When a person rests on himself, he easily turns to human comforts. But a true lover of Christ and a diligent seeker after virtue does not fall back on those comforts but desires great discipline and to undertake severe labors for Christ.

When, therefore, spiritual comfort is given by God, receive it with thanksgiving, and know that it is the gift of God, not what you deserve. Do not be lifted up, but rather be more humble for the gift, more careful in all you do. When comfort is taken from you, do not despair, but wait for the heavenly visitation with humility and patience, for God is able to give you back greater favor and consolation.

The psalmist said, when the favor of God was on him, "In my prosperity I said, 'I shall never be moved'" (Psalm 30:6), but he went on to say what he felt when the favor departed: "You hid Your face, and I was troubled" (Psalm 30:7). Yet he does not despair but instantly entreats God and says, "I cried out to You, O Lord, and to the Lord I made supplication" (Psalm 30:8). Then he received the answer to his prayer and testified how he had been heard, saying, "You have turned for me my mourning into dancing; You have put off my sackcloth and clothed me with gladness" (Psalm 30:11). If it was thus with the great saints, we who are poor and needy ought not despair if we are sometimes in the warmth and sometimes in the cold, for the Spirit comes and goes according to the good pleasure of His will.

What then can I hope and trust in except the great mercy of God and the hope of heavenly grace? For whether godly people are with me, faithful friends, holy books or beautiful discourses, sweet songs, all these help but little and have but little savor when I am deserted by

God's favor and left to my own poverty. There is no better remedy, then, than patience and denial of self and abiding in the will of God.

Divine comfort is given so that a man may be stronger to bear adversities. And temptation follows to keep him from being lifted up with pride. The devil does not sleep; your flesh is not yet dead; therefore, do not cease to make yourself ready for the battle, for enemies stand on your right hand and on your left, and they are never at rest.

CHAPTER 10

OF GRATITUDE FOR THE GRACE OF GOD

Why do you seek rest when you are born to labor? Prepare yourself for patience more than for comforts, and for bearing the cross more than for joy. Spiritual comforts exceed all the delights of the world and all the pleasures of the flesh. For all worldly delights are either empty or unclean, while spiritual delights alone are pleasant and honorable, the offspring of virtue, and poured forth by God into pure minds.

Always sit down in the lowest room and you will be given the highest place (Luke 14:10). For the highest saints of God are smallest in their own sight, and the more glorious they are, so much the lowlier are they in themselves. Resting on God and strong in His might, they cannot be lifted up in any way. They desire that God be praised above all things.

Be thankful, therefore, for the smallest benefit and you will be worthy to receive greater. God ever does for our profit whatever He allows to come upon us. He who seeks to retain the favor of God, let him be thankful for the favor that is given and patient about that which is taken away. Let him pray that it may return; let him be wary and humble that he lose it not.

CHAPTER 11

OF THE FEWNESS OF THOSE WHO LOVE THE CROSS OF JESUS

Jesus has many lovers of His heavenly kingdom but few bearers of His cross. He has many seekers of comfort but few of trials. He finds many companions of His table but few of His fasting. All desire to rejoice with Him, few are willing to undergo anything for His sake. Many follow Jesus that they may eat of His loaves, but few that they may drink of the cup of His passion. Many are astonished at His miracles, few follow after the shame of His cross. Many love Jesus so long as no adversities happen to them. Many praise Him and bless Him, so long as they receive comfort from Him. But if Jesus hides Himself and withdraws from them a little while, they fall into either complaining or depression.

But those who love Jesus for Jesus' sake bless Him in all tribulation and anguish of heart. And if He never gave them consolation, they would still praise Him and give Him thanks.

Chapter 12

Of the Royal Way of the Holy Cross

This seems a hard saying to many: "If anyone desires to come after Me, let him deny himself, and take up his cross, and follow Me" (Matthew 16:24). But it will be much harder to hear this sentence: "Depart from Me, you cursed, into the everlasting fire" (Matthew 25:41). For those who now willingly hear the word of the cross and follow it will not then fear the hearing of eternal damnation.

Why do you fear then to take up the cross that leads to a kingdom? In the cross is health, life, protection from enemies, heavenly sweetness, strength of mind, joy of the spirit, the height of virtue, perfection of holiness. There is no health of the soul, no hope of eternal life, apart from the cross. Take up your cross, therefore, and follow Jesus and you will go into eternal life. He went before you bearing His cross and died for you upon the cross so that you also may bear your cross and may love to be crucified upon it. For if you are dead with Him, you will also live with Him, and if you are a partaker of His sufferings, you will be also of His glory.

Everything depends on the cross, and everything lies in dying; and there is no other way to life and true inner peace than the way of the cross and daily dying to self.

Sometimes you will be forsaken of God, sometimes you will be tried by your neighbor, and you will often be wearisome to yourself. And still you cannot be delivered nor eased by any remedy or consolation, but must bear it as long as God wills. For God will have you learn to suffer trials without consolation, to submit yourself fully to them, and by them be made more humble. The cross is always ready and waits for you everywhere. You cannot flee from it, for wherever you go, you bring yourself with you and will ever find yourself and the cross.

If you willingly bear the cross, it will bear you and will bring you to the end you seek, where there will be an end to suffering, though it will not be here. If you bear it unwillingly, you make a burden for yourself and greatly increase your load, and yet you must bear it. If you cast away one cross, without doubt you will find another that will perhaps be heavier.

Do you think you will escape what no mortal has been able to avoid? Which of the saints in the world has been without the cross and trials? For not even Jesus Christ our Lord was one hour without the anguish of His passion. "It was necessary," He said, "for the Christ to suffer and to rise from the dead the third day" (Luke 24:46). And how do you seek another way than this royal way, which is the way of the holy cross?

The whole life of Christ was a cross and martyrdom, and do you seek for yourself rest and joy? You are wrong if you seek anything but to suffer trials, for this whole life is full of miseries and surrounded with crosses. And the higher a man has advanced in the spirit, the heavier crosses he will often find.

Yet the man who is thus afflicted in so many ways is not without refreshment of consolation, because he feels abundant fruit growing within him as a result of the bearing of his cross. For while he willingly submits himself to it, every burden of tribulation is turned into an assurance of divine comfort; and the more the flesh is weakened by affliction, the more is the spirit strengthened by inward grace. And often so greatly is he comforted by the desire for tribulation and adversity, through love of conformity to the cross of Christ, that he does not want to be without sorrow and tribulation, for he believes that he would be the more acceptable to God, the more and the heavier burdens he is able to bear for His sake.

It is not in the nature of man to bear the cross, to love the cross, to bring the body into subjection, to run from honors, to bear reproaches meekly, to despise self and desire to be despised, to bear all adversities and losses, and to desire no prosperity in this world. If you look to yourself, you will of yourself be able to do none of this; but if you trust in the Lord, endurance will be given you from heaven, and the world and the flesh will be made subject to your command. Indeed, you will not even fear your adversary the devil, if you are armed with faith and covered by the cross of Christ.

Set yourself, therefore, like a good and faithful servant of Christ to the courageous bearing of the cross of your Lord. Prepare yourself to bear many adversities and troubles in this life. There is no way to escape from trials and sorrow, except to bear them patiently. Lovingly drink your Lord's cup if you desire to be His friend. Leave consolations to God, let Him do as seems best to Him concerning them. "The sufferings of this present time are not worthy to be compared with the glory which shall be revealed in us" (Romans 8:18).

Oh, that you were worthy to suffer something for the name of Jesus, what great glory would await you, what rejoicing among all the saints of God, what bright example would you be to your neighbor! For all men commend patience, though few are willing to practice it.

If there had been anything better for people than to suffer, Christ would surely have shown it by word and example. For both the disciples who followed Him and all who desire to follow Him, He plainly exhorts to bear their cross, and says, "If anyone desires to come after Me, let him deny himself, and take up his cross daily, and follow Me" (Luke 9:23).

BOOK III
ON INWARD CONSOLATION

CHAPTER I
OF THE INWARD VOICE OF CHRIST

Blessed is the soul that hears the Lord speaking within it and receives the word of consolation from His mouth. Blessed are the ears that receive the echoes of the soft whisper of God and do not turn aside to the whisperings of this world. Blessed are the eyes that are closed to earthly things but are fixed on spiritual things. Blessed are those who long to have leisure for God and free themselves from every hindrance of the world.

These things says your Beloved, "I am your salvation, I am your peace and your life. Stay close to Me, and you will find peace." Put away all transitory things, seek those things that are eternal. For what are all temporal things but deceits, and how will all created things help you if you are forsaken by the Creator? Therefore put all other things away and give yourself to the Creator, to be well pleasing and faithful to Him.

CHAPTER 2

HOW ALL THE WORDS OF GOD ARE TO BE HEARD WITH HUMILITY

"My child, hear My words, for My words are most sweet, surpassing all the knowledge of the philosophers and wise men of this world. 'The words that I speak to you are spirit, and they are life' (John 6:63) and are not to be weighed by man's understanding. They are to be heard in silence and received with humility and deep love."

And I said, "Blessed is the man whom You instruct, O Lord, and teach out of Your law, that You may give him rest from the days of adversity" (Psalm 94:12–13).

"I," said the Lord, "taught the prophets from the beginning, and even now I do not cease to speak to all. But many are deaf and hardened against My voice; many love to listen to the world rather than to God. They follow after the desires of the flesh more readily than after the good pleasure of God. The world promises things that are temporal and small, and it is served with great eagerness. I promise things that are great and eternal, and the hearts of mortals are slow to stir. Who serves and obeys Me in all things with as much carefulness as he serves the world and its rulers? For a little reward men make a long journey; for eternal life many will hardly lift a foot off the ground.

"My promise fails no one, nor sends away empty him who trusts in Me. What I have promised I will give, what I have said I will fulfill, if only a man remain faithful in My love to the end. Therefore am I the rewarder of all good people and a strong approver of all who are godly.

"Write My words in your heart and consider them diligently, for you will need them in time of temptation. What you do not understand when you read, you will know when I come to you. I am accustomed to visit My elect in a twofold manner: by temptation and by comfort, and I teach them two lessons day by day, the one in chastising their faults, the other in exhorting them to grow in grace."

O Lord my God, I am the very poorest of Your servants. I am nothing, I have nothing, and can do nothing. You only are good, just, and holy; You can do all things, are over all things, fill all things, leaving empty only the sinner. Remember Your tender mercies and fill my heart with Your grace.

How can I bear this life unless Your merc. and grace strengthen me? Do not turn Your face away from me. Withdraw not Your comfort from me. Lord, teach me to do Your will, teach me to walk humbly and uprightly before You, for You are my wisdom.

CHAPTER 3

HOW WE MUST WALK IN TRUTH AND HUMILITY BEFORE GOD

"My child, walk before Me in truth, and in the simplicity of your heart seek Me continually. He who walks before Me in the truth will be safe from evil, and the truth will deliver him from the tricks and slanders of the wicked. If the truth shall make you free, you shall be free indeed, and will not care for the meaningless words of men."

Lord, let Your truth teach me, let it keep me and preserve me to the end. Let it free me from all evil and lust, and I will walk before You in great freedom of heart.

"I will teach you," says the Truth, "the things that are right and pleasing before Me. Think on your sins with great displeasure and sorrow, and never think yourself anything because of your good works. Truly you are a sinner, prone to many passions. Of yourself you always tend to nothing and will quickly fall, quickly be conquered, quickly disturbed, quickly undone. You have nothing in which to glory, but many reasons why you should reckon yourself vile, for you are far weaker than you can comprehend.

"Let nothing that you do, therefore, seem great to you; let nothing be grand, of value or beauty, worthy of honor, lofty, or desirable except what is eternal. Let the eternal truth please you above all things. Flee from nothing so much as your own faults and sins.

"Fear the judgments of God. Shrink from debating about the works of the Most High, but consider what great sins you have fallen into and how many good things you have neglected. There are some who carry their devotion only in books, and some have Me in their mouths but little in their hearts. Others there are who continually long after eternal things. These understand what the Spirit of truth speaks in them, for He teaches them to despise earthly things and to love heavenly; to neglect the world and to desire heaven day and night."

CHAPTER 4

OF THE WONDERFUL POWER
OF THE DIVINE LOVE

I bless You, O heavenly Father, that You have stooped to think of me, poor as I am. I give thanks to You, who refreshes me sometimes with Your own comfort when I am unworthy of any comfort. I bless and glorify You continually, with Your only begotten Son and the Holy Spirit, forever and ever. O Lord God, lover of my soul, when You will come into my heart, my inner being will rejoice. You are my glory and the joy of my heart. You are my hope and my refuge in the day of trouble.

But because I am still weak in love and imperfect in virtue, I need to be strengthened and comforted by You; therefore visit me often and instruct me with Your holy ways of discipline. Deliver me from evil passions, and cleanse my heart from all ungodly desires, that I may be made ready to love, strong to suffer, steadfast to endure.

Love is a great thing, making every heavy burden light and equalizing every inequality. For it bears the burden and makes every bitter thing sweet. The surpassing love of Jesus compels us to great works and motivates us to desire greater perfection. Love wills to be free from all worldly affection, lest its inward power of vision be hindered, lest it be entangled by any worldly prosperity or overcome by adversity. Nothing is sweeter than love, nothing stronger, nothing loftier, nothing broader, nothing more pleasant, nothing better in heaven or on earth.

He who loves runs and is glad; he is free and unhindered. He looks not for gifts but turns himself to the Giver above all good things. Love feels no burden, is not bothered by work, strives after more than it is able to do, considers nothing impossible, because it judges possible all things that are lawful for it. It is strong for all things and fulfills many things, and it is successful where he who does not love fails.

Love is watchful; though fatigued it is not weary, though compelled it is not forced, though alarmed it is not terrified. The ardent affection of the soul is a beautiful noise in the ears of God, and it says: "My God, my Beloved! You are all mine, and I am all Yours."

Enlarge me in love, that I may learn how sweet it is to love, to be dissolved, and to swim in love. Let me be held by love. Let me sing the song of love, let me follow You on high, let my soul exhaust itself in Your praise, exulting with love. Let me love You more than myself.

Love is swift, sincere, virtuous, pleasant, gentle, strong, patient, faithful, prudent, long-suffering, and never seeking its own; for where ever a man seeks his own, there he falls from love. Love is circumspect, humble, and upright; not weak, not fickle, nor intent on meaningless things, sober, undefiled, steadfast, quiet, and guarded. Love is obedient to all who are in authority, humble in its own sight, devout and grateful toward God, faithful and always trusting in Him even when He hides His face.

He who is not ready to suffer all things and to conform to the will of the Beloved is not worthy to be called a lover of God. It is necessary for him who loves to willingly embrace all hard things for the Beloved's sake, and not to be drawn away from Him by any hardship.

CHAPTER 5

OF THE PROVING
OF THE TRUE LOVER

"My child, you are not yet strong and prudent in your love."

Why, O my Lord?

"Because when there is a little opposition you fall away from your undertakings and too eagerly seek consolation. The strong lover stands fast in temptations and believes not the evil persuasions of the enemy. As in prosperity I please him, so in adversity I do not displease.

"The wise lover considers not the gift of the lover so much as the love of the giver. The noble lover rests not in the gift, but in Me above every gift.

"All is not lost, though you sometimes think of Me less often than you should desire. That sweet affection that you sometimes perceive is the effect of grace and a foretaste of the heavenly country, but you must not depend on it too much, for it comes and goes. But to strive against sinful thoughts and resist the suggestions of the devil is a sign of virtue.

"Know that your old enemy strives to hinder

your pursuit after good and to distract you from every godly discipline. He suggests to you many evil thoughts, that he may work in you weariness and terror and so draw you away from prayer and Bible reading. Humble confession displeases him. Do not listen to him. Say to him, 'Depart, detestable deceiver. You will have no part in me, but Jesus will be with me, as a strong warrior. I would rather die and bear all suffering than consent to you. I will not hear you anymore, though you plot more snares against me. "The Lord is my light and my salvation; whom shall I fear? Though an army may encamp against me, my heart shall not fear. . .O Lord, my strength and my Redeemer"' (Psalms 27:1, 3; 19:14).

"Strive like a good soldier; and if sometimes you fail through weakness, put on your strength more bravely than before, trusting in My more abundant grace, and watch out for self-confidence and pride."

CHAPTER 6

OF HIDING OUR GRACE UNDER THE GUARD OF HUMILITY

"There are many who, when things have not gone well for them, become impatient or slothful. 'The way of man is not in himself' (Jeremiah 10:23), but it is God's place to console when He will, as much as He will, and whom He will. Some who were presumptuous because of the grace of devotion within them have destroyed themselves, because they did more than they were able, not considering their own weakness but following the impulses of their hearts rather than the judgment of reason. And because they presumed beyond what was well-pleasing to God, they quickly lost grace. They became poor and were left in sin, so that being humbled and stricken with poverty of spirit, they might learn not to fly with their own wings but to put their trust under My feathers. Those who are as yet new and unskilled in the ways of the Lord may easily be deceived and led away unless they rule themselves after the counsel of the wise.

"But if they wish to follow their own fancy rather than trust the experience of others, the result will be very dangerous to them. Those who are wise in their own eyes seldom patiently endure being ruled by others. It is better to have a small portion of wisdom with humility and a little understanding than great treasures of knowledge with an inflated ego. It is better for you to have less than to have much of what may make you proud. He who gives himself entirely to joy is unwise, forgetting his former helplessness and the fear of the Lord. Nor is he very wise who in time of adversity bears himself too despairingly and feels less trusting of Me than he ought.

"If you knew how to continue to be humble and rule your own spirit well, you would not so quickly fall into danger and mischief. It is good counsel that when fervor of spirit is kindled, you should meditate how it will be with you when the light is taken away. When that does happen, remember that the light will return again, which I have taken away for a time as a warning, and also for My own glory. Such a trial is often more useful than if things were always prosperous according to your will."

CHAPTER 7

OF A LOW ESTIMATION OF
SELF IN THE SIGHT OF GOD

I, who am but dust and ashes, will speak to my Lord. If I consider myself more than this, You stand against me. But if I humble myself and bring myself to nothing, Your grace will be favorable to me and Your light will be near my heart, and my ego, however small it might be, will be swallowed up in the depths of my nothingness and perish forever. There You show me myself, what I am, what I was, and where I have come from: "I was so foolish and ignorant" (Psalm 73:22). If I am left to myself, I am nothing, I am all weakness; but if suddenly You look upon me, immediately I am made strong and filled with new joy.

By loving myself, I lost myself; and by seeking and sincerely loving You alone, I found both myself and You, because You deal with me beyond anything I deserve.

You are blessed, O my God, because though I am unworthy of all Your benefits, Your bountiful and infinite goodness never ceases to do good even to those who are turned far from You. Turn us to Yourself, that we may be grateful, humble, and godly, for You are our salvation, our courage, and our strength.

CHAPTER 8

THAT ALL THINGS ARE
TO BE REFERRED TO GOD

"My child, I must be your supreme and final goal, if you desire to be truly happy. Out of such purpose your affection will be purified, which too often is sinfully bent upon itself and created things. For if you seek yourself in any matter, immediately you will fail within yourself and grow barren. Therefore refer everything to Me first of all, for it is I who gave you all.

"From Me the humble and great, the poor and the rich, draw water as from a living fountain, and those who serve Me with a free and faithful spirit will receive grace. But he who glories apart from Me will not be established in true joy nor enlarged in heart, but will be greatly hindered and thrown into tribulation. Therefore you must not credit any good to yourself, nor look on virtue as belonging to any person, but credit it all to God. I gave all, I will receive all again, and I require the giving of thanks.

"If heavenly grace and true love enter into you, there will be no envy, nor stinginess of the heart, nor will any self-love take possession of you. For divine love conquers all things and enlarges the soul. If you are truly wise, you will rejoice in Me alone, you will hope in Me alone; for 'no one is good but One, that is, God' (Luke 18:19), who is to be praised above all things, and in all things to receive blessing."

CHAPTER 9

THAT IT IS SWEET TO DESPISE THE WORLD AND TO SERVE GOD

"Oh, how great is Your goodness, which You have laid up for those who fear You!" (Psalm 31:19). But what are You to those who love You and serve You with their whole heart? Truly unspeakable is the sweetness of the contemplation of You. In this most of all You have shown me the sweetness of Your love: that You made me, and when I wandered far from You, You brought me back that I might serve You, and commanded me to love You.

O fountain of perpetual love, what will I say concerning You, who condescended to remember me, even after I pined away and perished? You have had mercy beyond all hope on Your servant and have shown Your grace and friendship beyond all deserving. What reward will I render You for Your grace? For it is not given to all to renounce this world and its affairs, and to take up a religious life. For it is a great thing that I should serve You, whom every creature ought to serve. It ought not to seem a great thing to me to serve You; but rather this appears to me a great and wonderful thing, that You receive as Your servant one so poor and unworthy and join him to Your chosen servants.

Everything I have is Yours, and with it all I serve You. And yet truly it is You who serves me, rather than I You. Look at the heaven and earth You have created for the service of men; they are at Your bidding and perform daily whatever You command. And this is a small thing, for You have even ordained the angels for the service of man. But it surpasses even all these things, that You Yourself minister to man, and promised that You would give Yourself to him.

What shall I give back to You for all Your mercies? Oh, that I were able to serve You all the days of my life! Oh, that even for one day I were enabled to do You service worthy of Yourself! For truly You are worthy of all service, all honor, and praise without end. You are my God, and I am Your poor servant, who am bound to serve You with all my strength, nor ought I ever to grow weary of Your praise.

It is great honor and glory to serve You. For those who submit themselves to Your most holy service will have great grace. Those who for love of You have laid aside every carnal delight will find the sweetest consolation of the Holy Spirit. Those who enter the narrow way of life for Your name's sake, and have put away all worldly cares, will attain great liberty of spirit.

CHAPTER 10

THAT THE DESIRES OF THE HEART ARE TO BE EXAMINED AND GOVERNED

"My child, you still have many things to learn."

What are they, Lord?

"To place your desire altogether in subjection to My good pleasure, and not to be a lover of yourself but an earnest seeker of My will. Your desires often excite and urge you forward; but consider whether you are not moved more for your own ends than for My honor. If it is Myself that you seek, you will be content with whatever I ordain; but if any pursuit of your own lies hidden within you, it hinders and weighs you down.

"Beware, therefore, that you not strive too earnestly after some desire that you have conceived without taking counsel of Me, lest you regret it afterwards and that which before pleased you now displease you. For not everything that seems good is to be followed, neither is every negative thing to be immediately avoided. Sometimes it is expedient to use restraint even in good desires and wishes, lest through importunity you fall into distraction of mind, lest through lack of discipline you become a stumbling block to others, or lest by the resistance of others you be suddenly disturbed and brought to confusion.

"Sometimes it is necessary to courageously strive against the sensual appetite, and not to consider what the flesh may or not want, that it may become subject, however unwillingly, to the spirit. And it ought to be chastised and compelled to undergo slavery until it is ready for all things and has learned to be contented with little, to be delighted with simple things, and never to murmur at any inconvenience."

CHAPTER 11

OF THE INWARD GROWTH OF PATIENCE

O Lord God, I see that patience is very necessary for me, for many things in this life go contrary to my wishes. For however I may have contrived for my peace, my life cannot go on without strife and trouble.

"You speak truthfully, My child. For I do not want you to seek a peace that is without trials, but rather that you should consider yourself to have found peace when you are tried and proven by many adversities. Strive on God's behalf to endure hardships bravely. Do you think that the children of this world suffer nothing or just a little? You will not find it so, even among the most prosperous.

" 'But,' you may say, 'they have many delights, and they follow their own wills, and thus they bear lightly their tribulations.'

"They may have what they want, but how long do you think it will last? Like smoke those who are rich in this world will pass away, and no record will remain of their past joys. Even while they live, they do not rest without bitterness and weariness and fear. For from the very same thing in which they find delight, in that they often have the punishment of sorrow. Justly it befalls them, because they pursue pleasures and enjoy them not without confusion and bitterness. Oh how short, how false, how wicked are all these pleasures! Yet because of their drunkenness and blindness men do not understand; but like beasts, for the sake of a little pleasure, they incur death on their souls.

"If you want to find true delight and be abundantly comforted of Me, hold in contempt all worldly things and avoid all worthless pleasures. And the more you withdraw yourself from the solace of people, the more sweet and powerful consolations will you find. But at first you will not attain to them without some sorrow and hard striving. Long-accustomed habits will oppose, but they will be overcome by better habits. The flesh will murmur again and again but will be restrained by fervor of spirit. The devil will push you but will be put to flight by prayer."

Chapter 12

Of the Obedience of One in Lowly Subjection

"My child, he who strives to withdraw himself from obedience withdraws himself also from grace. If a man does not submit willingly to one set over him, it is a sign that his flesh is not yet perfectly subject to himself but it often resists. Learn therefore to quickly submit yourself to him who is over you if you seek to bring your flesh into subjection. There is no more grievous and deadly enemy to the soul than you are to yourself, if you are not led by the Spirit. As yet you love yourself too much, therefore you shrink from yielding yourself to the will of others.

"But what great thing is it that you, who are dust and nothingness, yield yourself to man for God's sake, when I, the Most High, who created all things out of nothing, subjected Myself to man for your sake? I became the most humble and despised of men, that by My humility you might overcome your pride. Learn to obey! Learn to humble yourself and to bow yourself beneath the feet of all. Learn to crush your passions and to yield yourself in all subjection.

"Be zealous against yourself and do not allow pride to live within you, but show yourself as being of no reputation. What do you have about which to complain? What can you answer those who speak against you, seeing you have so often offended God? But My eye has spared you, because your soul was precious in My sight; that you might know My love and might be thankful for My benefits; and that you might give yourself to true humility."

CHAPTER 13

OF MEDITATION ON THE HIDDEN JUDGMENTS OF GOD

There is no holiness if You, O Lord, withdraw Your hand. No wisdom profits if You stop guiding the helm. No strength avails if You cease to preserve. No purity is secure if You protect it not. No self-keeping avails if Your holy watching is not there. For when we are left alone we are swallowed up and perish, but when we are visited, we are raised up and we live. For indeed we are unstable but are made strong through You; we grow cold but are rekindled by You.

Chapter 14

How We Must Stand and Speak in Everything We Desire

"My child, speak this way in every matter: 'Lord, if it please You, let this come to pass. If this will be for Your honor, let it be done in Your name. If You see that it is good and useful for me, then grant me to use it for Your honor. But if You know that it will be harmful to the health of my soul, take the desire away from me!' For not every desire is from the Holy Spirit, although it appear to a man right and good. It is difficult to judge with certainty whether a good or bad spirit moves you to desire this or that, or whether you are moved by your own spirit.

"Therefore, whatever seems to you desirable, you must always seek after it with the fear of God and humility of heart and, most of all, must completely surrender yourself and commit all to Me and say, 'Lord, You know what is best; let this or that be, according as You will. Give what You will, as much as You will, when You will. Do with me as You know best, and as will best please You, and as will be most to Your honor. Place me where You will and freely work Your will in me in all things. I am in Your hand. I am Your servant, ready for all things; for I desire to live not for myself but for You.'"

A Prayer to Be Enabled to Do God's Will Perfectly

Grant me Your grace, most merciful Jesus, that it may be with me, and work in me, and persevere with me, even to the end. Grant that I may ever desire whatever is most pleasing and dear to You. Let Your will be mine, and let my will always follow Yours. May I choose and reject whatever You choose and reject; indeed, let it be impossible for me to choose or reject anything except according to Your will.

Grant that I may die to all worldly things, and for Your sake love to be despised and unknown in this world. Grant to me to rest in You, and that in You my heart may be at peace. You are the true peace of the heart, You alone its rest; apart from You all things are hard and unsettled. In You alone, the supreme and eternal God, "I will both lie down in peace and sleep" (Psalm 4:8). Amen.

CHAPTER 15

THAT TRUE COMFORT IS
TO BE SOUGHT IN GOD ALONE

Whatever I desire for my comfort, I do not look for it here but hereafter. For if I had all the comforts of this world and were able to enjoy all its delights, it is certain that they could not last long. Therefore, my soul, you can be fully comforted and perfectly refreshed only in God, the comforter of the poor and the lifter up of the humble. Wait a little while, my soul, wait for the divine promise, and you will have abundance of all good things in heaven. If you long too much for the things that are now, you will lose those that are eternal and heavenly. Let temporal things be in the use, eternal things in the desire. You cannot be satisfied with any temporal good, for you were not created for the enjoyment of these.

Even if you had all the good things that were ever created, you could not be happy and blessed; all your blessedness and your happiness lie in God, who created all things. All human comfort is empty and short-lived; blessed and true is the comfort that is felt inwardly, springing from the truth. Everywhere he goes, the godly man carries with himself his own Comforter, Jesus, and says to Him: "Be with me, Lord Jesus, always and everywhere. Let it be my comfort to be able to give up cheerfully all human comfort. And if Your consolations fail me, let Your will and righteous approval be always with me for the highest comfort. For You will not always strive with us, nor will You keep Your anger forever" (see Psalm 103:9).

Chapter 16

That All Care Is to Be Cast on God

"My child, allow Me to do with you what I will; I know what is best for you. You think as a man, in many things you judge as human affection persuades you."

Lord, what You say is true. Greater is Your care for me than all the care that I am able to take for myself. For too insecurely does he stand who does not cast all his care on You. Lord, as long as my will stands right and firm in You, do with me what You will, for whatever You will do with me cannot be anything but good. You are blessed if You leave me in darkness; You are also blessed if You leave me in light. You are blessed if You comfort me, and always blessed if You cause me to be troubled.

"My child! This is how you must stand if you desire to walk with Me. You must be ready for suffering and rejoicing alike. You must be poor and needy as willingly as full and rich."

Lord, I will willingly bear for You whatever You will have come upon me. I will receive from Your hand good and evil, sweet and bitter, joy and sadness, and will give You thanks for all things that happen to me. Keep me from all sin, and I will not fear death or hell.

Chapter 17

That Temporal Miseries Are to Be Borne Patiently

"My child! I came down from heaven for your salvation; I took upon Myself your miseries not because I had to but because I was drawn by love that you might learn patience and might bear earthly hardships without murmuring. For from the hour of My birth until My death on the cross, I never stopped bearing sorrow; I lacked many temporal things; I often heard many reproaches against Myself; I gently bore contradictions and hard words; I received ingratitude for benefits, blasphemies for My miracles, rebukes for My doctrine."

Lord, because You were patient in Your life, herein most of all fulfilling the commandment of Your Father, it is well that I, a miserable sinner, should patiently bear myself according to Your will. For although this present life seems burdensome, it is nevertheless made full of merit through Your grace, and to those who are weak it becomes easier and brighter through Your example.

Oh, what great thanks am I bound to give

You for showing me and all faithful people the good and right way to Your eternal kingdom. If You had not gone before us and taught us, who would care to follow? Oh, how far would they have gone backward if they had not seen Your glorious example! We are still lukewarm, though we have heard of Your many signs and discourses; what would become of us if we did not have such a light to help us follow You?

Chapter 18

Of Bearing Hardships

"What do you say, My child? Cease to complain; consider My sufferings and those of My saints. 'You have not yet resisted to bloodshed' (Hebrews 12:4). You suffer little compared to those who have suffered so many things, have been so strongly tempted, so grievously troubled, so tried and proven. You ought therefore to consider the more grievous sufferings of others that you might bear your lesser ones more easily, and if they do not seem little to you, see that it is not your impatience that is the cause. But whether they are little or great, learn to bear them all with patience.

"So far as you set yourself to bear patiently, so far you do wisely. You will also bear things more easily if your mind and habit are carefully trained that way. And do not say, 'I cannot bear these things from such a person, for he has done me grievous harm and accused me of something I never thought of. But from another I will suffer patiently such things as I see I ought to suffer.' Foolish is such a thought as this, for it considers not the virtue of patience, nor by whom that virtue is to be crowned, but it rather weighs the persons and offences against self.

"He is not truly patient who will only suffer as far as seems right to himself and from whom he pleases. But the truly patient person considers not by what person he is tried, but from every creature, whatever or however often adversity happens to him, he gratefully accepts all from the hand of God and considers it great gain. For with God nothing that is borne for His sake, however small, will lose its reward.

"Be therefore ready for the fight if you desire the victory. Without striving you cannot win the crown of patience; if you will not suffer you refuse to be crowned. But if you desire to be crowned, strive bravely, endure patiently. Without labor you do not draw near rest, nor without fighting can you come to victory."

Make possible to me, O Lord, by grace what seems impossible to me by nature. You know how little I am able to bear and how quickly I am cast down when a similar adversity rises up against me. Whatever trial may come to me, may it become to me pleasing and acceptable, for to suffer for Your sake is very good for the soul.

CHAPTER 19

OF CONFESSION
OF OUR WEAKNESS

I will acknowledge my sin to You (see Psalm 32:5), I will confess to You, Lord, my weakness. It is often a small thing that casts me down and makes me sad. I resolve that I will act bravely, but when a little temptation comes, immediately I am in great distress.

Behold, therefore, O Lord, my humility and my frailty, which You already know. Be merciful to me, and draw me out of the mire (see Psalm 69:14), or I will remain discouraged. What frequently discourages me is that I am so prone to fall, so weak to resist my passions. And though their assault is not altogether according to my will, it is violent and grievous, and it wearies me to live in daily conflict. Hateful fantasies always rush in far more easily than they depart.

Oh, that You, most mighty God of Israel, Lover of all faithful souls, would look upon the labor and sorrow of Your servant and give him help in all things about which he strives. Strengthen me, lest this miserable flesh, not yet being fully subdued to the spirit, should rule over me. Oh, what a life is this, where tribulations and miseries do not cease, where all things are full of snares and enemies, for when one trial or temptation goes, another comes.

And how can the life of man be loved, seeing that it has so many bitter things, that it is subjected to so many calamities and miseries? How can it even be called life, when it produces so many deaths and plagues? The world is often reproached because it is deceitful and vain, yet notwithstanding it is not easily given up, because the lusts of the flesh have too much rule over it. Some draw us to love, some to hate. The lust of the flesh, the lust of the eyes, and the pride of life, these draw to love of the world; but the punishments and miseries that righteously follow these things bring forth hatred of the world and weariness.

Those who perfectly despise the world and strive to live for God in holy discipline are not ignorant of the divine sweetness promised to all who truly deny themselves and see clearly how grievously the world errs and in how many ways it is deceived.

Chapter 20

That We Must Rest in God above All Goods and Gifts

Above all things and in all things you will rest always in the Lord, O my soul, for He Himself is the eternal rest of the saints. Grant me, sweet Jesus, to rest in You above every creature, above all health and beauty, above all glory and honor, above all power and dignity, above all knowledge and skillfulness, above all riches and arts, above all joy and exultation, above all fame and praise, above all sweetness and consolation, above all hope and promise, above all gifts that You can give, above all joy the mind is able to receive; above everything that You, O my God, are not.

For You, O Lord, are best above all things; You only are the Most High, You only the Almighty, You only the all-sufficient and fullness of all things; You only the all-delightful and all-comforting; You alone the altogether lovely and altogether loving; You alone the Most Exalted and Most Glorious above all things; in whom all things are, and were, and ever shall be. And thus it is insufficient whatever You give me without

Yourself or whatever You reveal or promise concerning Yourself, while You are not seen or fully possessed, since my heart cannot truly rest or be entirely content unless it rests in You.

Most holy lover of my soul, ruler of this whole creation, who will give me the wings of true liberty, that I may fly to You and find rest? When will it be given me to be open to receive You to the full and to see how sweet You are? When will I lose myself altogether in You, that because of Your love I may not feel myself at all, but may know You. But now I often groan and bear my sad state with sorrow, because many evils befall me that continually disturb me and continually fill me with care, allure and entangle me, that I cannot have free access to You, nor enjoy sweet communion with You.

O Jesus, light of eternal glory, comfort of the wandering soul, before You my mouth is without speech, and my silence speaks to You. How long will my Lord delay to come to me? Let Him come to me, His poor and humble one, and make me glad. Let Him deliver His holy one from every snare. Come, for without You there will be no joyful day or hour, for You are my joy, and without You is my table empty. I am miserable and imprisoned until You refresh me by the light of Your presence and give me liberty and show Your loving countenance.

Let others seek things other than You, but for me nothing pleases or will please except You, my God, my hope, my eternal salvation. I will not be quiet nor cease to implore until your grace returns and You speak to me.

"Behold, here I am! Behold, I come to you, for you called Me. Your tears and the longing of your soul, your humbleness and contrition of heart have beckoned Me and brought Me to you."

And I said, Lord, I have called on You, and I have longed to enjoy You, being ready to reject everything for Your sake. For You first moved me to seek You. Therefore, You are blessed, O Lord, who has wrought this good work on Your servant, according to the multitude of Your mercy. What then has Your servant to say in Your presence, except to humble himself greatly before You, being always mindful of his own iniquity. For there is none like You in heaven and earth. Excellent are Your works, true are Your judgments, and by Your providence are all things governed. Therefore praise and glory be to You; let my mouth and my soul and all created things praise and bless You together.

CHAPTER 21

OF THE RECOLLECTION OF GOD'S MANIFOLD BENEFITS

Open my heart, O Lord, in Your law, and teach me to walk in the way of Your commandments. Help me to understand Your will and remember Your benefits with great reverence and diligent meditation, that I may be worthy to give You thanks. Yet I know and confess that I cannot render You due praises for the least of Your mercies. I am less than the least of all the good things that you gave me, and when I consider Your majesty, my spirit fails because of the greatness thereof.

All things we have in the soul and in the body, and whatever things we possess, whether naturally or spiritually, are Your good gifts and prove You to be good, gentle, and kind. Although one receives many things, and another fewer, yet all are Yours, and without You not even the smallest thing can be possessed. He who has received greater cannot boast that it is of his own merit, nor lift himself up above others, nor scorn those beneath him; for he is the greater and the better who credits least to himself, and in giving thanks is the humbler and more devout.

But he who has received fewer gifts ought not to be discouraged nor take it wrong nor envy him who is richer; but rather he ought to look to You and greatly praise Your goodness, for You pour out Your gifts so richly and freely, without respect of persons. All things come from You, therefore in all things will You be praised. You know what is best to be given to each.

Nothing ought to give so much joy to him who loves You as Your will in him and the good pleasure of Your eternal providence, wherewith he ought to be so contented and comforted that he would as willingly be the least as any other would be the greatest, as peaceable and contented in the lowest as in the highest place, and as willingly held of small and low account and of no reputation as to be more honorable and greater in the world than others. For Your will and the love of Your honor ought to go before all things.

CHAPTER 22

FOUR THINGS THAT BRING GREAT PEACE

"My child, now will I teach you the way of peace and true liberty."

Do as You say, O my Lord, for this is pleasing to me to hear.

"Strive, My child, to do another's will rather than your own. Choose always to have less rather than more. Seek always after the lowest place and to be subject to all. Wish always and pray that the will of God be fulfilled in you. Such a person as this enters into the inheritance of peace and quietness."

O my Lord, this Your discourse is short in words but full of meaning and abundant in fruit. For if it were possible that I should fully keep it, I would not be so easily disturbed. For as often as I feel myself upset and weighed down, I find myself to have gone back from this teaching. But You, who always love progress in the soul, give more grace, that I may be enabled to fulfill Your exhortation and work out my salvation.

A Prayer against Evil Thoughts

"O God, do not be far from me; O my God, make haste to help me!" (Psalm 71:12), for many thoughts and great fears have risen up against me, afflicting my soul. How will I pass through them unharmed? How will I break through them?

" 'I will go before you, and make the crooked places straight' (Isaiah 45:2). I will open the prison doors and reveal to you the secret places."

Do as You say, Lord, and let all evil thoughts fly away before Your face. This is my hope and my only comfort, to fly to You in the midst of all trials, to hope in You, to call on You from my heart and patiently wait for Your lovingkindness.

A Prayer for Enlightenment of the Mind

Enlighten me, Jesus, with the brightness of Your inner light, and cast out all darkness from my heart. Restrain my many wandering thoughts, and carry away the temptations that strive to do me harm. Fight mightily for me, and drive forth the evil beasts—alluring lusts—that "peace be within [my] walls, prosperity within [my] palaces" (Psalm 122:7), even in my pure conscience. Command the winds and the storms, say to the sea, "Be still," say to the stormy wind, "Hold your peace."

"Oh, send out Your light and Your truth!" (Psalm 43:3), that they may shine on the earth, for I am but earth without form and void until You give me light. Pour forth Your grace from above; water my heart with the dew of heaven; give the waters of devotion to water the face of the earth, and cause it to bring forth good and perfect fruit. Lift up my mind, which is oppressed with the weight of sins, and raise my whole desire to heavenly things, that having tasted the sweetness of the happiness that is from above, it may take no pleasure in thinking of things of earth.

Draw me and deliver me from every unstable comfort of creatures, for no created thing is able to satisfy my desire and to give me comfort. Join me to Yourself by the inseparable bond of love, for You alone are sufficient to him who loves You, and without You all things are vain toys.

CHAPTER 23

OF AVOIDING INQUIRY INTO THE LIFE OF ANOTHER

"My child, do not be curious about others or trouble yourself with meaningless cares. 'What is that to you? You follow Me' (John 21:22). For what is it to you whether a man is this or that or says or does such and such? You have no need to answer for others, but you must give an answer for yourself. Why therefore do you entangle yourself? I know all men, and I see all things that are done under the sun; and I know how each one thinks, what he wills, and to what end his thoughts reach. All things therefore are to be committed to Me; watch yourself in godly peace, and leave him who is disturbed to be disturbed as he will.

"Trouble not yourself about the shadow of a great name, nor about the friendship of many, nor about the love of people toward you. For these things generate distraction and great sorrows of heart. My Word should speak freely to you, and I would reveal secrets if only you diligently looked for My appearing and opened to Me the gates of your heart. 'Be serious and watchful in your prayers' (1 Peter 4:7), and humble yourself in all things."

CHAPTER 24

WHEREIN FIRM PEACE OF HEART AND TRUE PROFIT CONSIST

"My child, I have said, 'Peace I leave with you, My peace I give to you; not as the world gives do I give to you' (John 14:27). All men desire peace, but all do not care for the things that belong to true peace. My peace is with the humble and lowly in heart. Your peace will be in much patience. If you heard Me and followed My voice, you would enjoy much peace."

What then shall I do, Lord?

"In everything be careful about what you do and what you say, and direct all your purpose into pleasing Me alone, and desire and seek nothing apart from Me. Moreover, judge nothing rashly concerning the words or deeds of others, nor meddle with matters that are not yours; and it may be that you will be disturbed little or rarely. Yet never to feel any anxiety nor to suffer any pain of heart or body does not belong to the present life but to the state of eternal rest. Therefore do not consider yourself to have found true peace if you have felt no grief; nor that all is well if you have no adversary; nor that things are perfect when they go according to your desire. And do not consider yourself to be anything great or think that you are specially beloved if you are in a state of great fervor and sweetness of spirit; for not by these things is the true lover of virtue known, nor in them does the profit and perfection of man consist."

In what then, Lord?

"In offering yourself with all your heart to the divine will, in not seeking the things that are your own, whether great or small, whether temporal or eternal, so that you remain steady in giving of thanks between prosperity and adversity, weighing all things in an equal balance. If you are brave and long-suffering in hope even when inner comfort is taken from you, you prepare your heart for greater endurance and do not justify yourself, as though you should not have to suffer these heavy things, but you justify Me in all things that I appoint and bless My holy name, then you walk in the true and right way of peace and will have a sure hope that you will again see My face with joy. For if you come to an utter contempt of yourself, know that then you will enjoy abundance of peace, as much as is possible while you are here on earth."

CHAPTER 25

OF THE EXALTATION
OF A FREE SPIRIT

I beseech You, my most merciful Lord God, preserve me from the cares of this life, that I not become too entangled; from many necessities of the body, that I not get taken captive by pleasure; from all obstacles of the spirit, that I not be broken and cast down with cares.

O my God, sweetness unspeakable, turn into bitterness all my carnal consolations, which draw me away from the love of eternal things. O my God, let not flesh and blood prevail over me, let not the world and its short glory deceive me, let not the devil and his craftiness overtake me. Give me courage to resist, patience to endure, constancy to persevere. Grant, in place of all consolations of the world, the sweet anointing of Your Spirit, and in place of carnal love, pour into me the love of Your name.

Food and drink and clothing, and all the other needs pertaining to the support of the body, are burdensome to the devout spirit. Grant that I may use such things with moderation and not be entangled with inordinate love for them. To cast away all these things is not lawful, because nature must be sustained, but to require things that merely minister delight the holy law forbids. For otherwise the flesh would become insolent against the spirit. In all these things I beseech You, let Your hand guide and teach me.

CHAPTER 26

THAT PERSONAL LOVE GREATLY HINDERS FROM THE HIGHEST GOOD

"My child, you must be nothing of your own. Know that the love of yourself is more harmful to you than anything in the world. According to the love and inclination you have, everything more or less clings to you. If your love be pure and sincere, you will not be in captivity to anything. Do not covet what you may not have; do not have what is able to rob you of inner liberty.

"Why are you wearied with superfluous cares? Stand by My good pleasure, and you will suffer no loss. If you seek after this or that and want to be here or there, according to your own advantage or the fulfilling of your own pleasure, you will never be at peace or free from care, because in everything something will be found lacking, and everywhere there will be somebody who opposes you.

"Therefore it is not the multiplying of this thing or that that benefits you, but rather the despising of it and cutting it by the root out of your heart. This includes not only money and riches but the desire for honor and meaningless praise. The peace that is sought apart from Me will not last long if the state of your heart is without the true foundation, that is, if it abide not in Me. You may change, but you cannot better yourself."

A Prayer for Cleansing of the Heart and for Heavenly Wisdom

Strengthen me, O God, by the grace of Your Holy Spirit. Give me virtue to be strengthened inwardly and to free my heart from all fruitless care and trouble, and that I not be drawn away by various desires after any things at all, but that I may look upon all as passing away, and myself as passing away with them.

Give me, O Lord, heavenly wisdom, that I may learn to seek You above all things and to find You; to relish You above all things and to love You; and to understand all other things according to the order of Your wisdom. Help me to prudently avoid the flatterer and patiently bear with him who opposes me.

CHAPTER 27

AGAINST THE TONGUES OF DETRACTORS

"My child, do not take it to heart if any think poorly of you and say of you what you are unwilling to hear. You ought to think worse of yourself and to believe no man weaker than yourself. It is no small prudence to keep silence in an evil time and to turn to Me and not to be troubled by human judgment.

"Let not your peace depend on the word of people, for whether they judge well or poorly of you, you are not any other person than yourself. Where is true peace or true glory? Is it not in Me? And he who seeks not to please men, nor fears to displease, will enjoy abundant peace."

CHAPTER 28

WHEN TRIBULATION COMES

Blessed be Your name forever, O Lord, who has willed this temptation and trouble to come upon me. I cannot escape it but have need to flee to You, that You may help me and turn it for my good. It is not well within my heart, but I am vexed by suffering. "Save Me from this hour. . . but for this purpose I came to this hour" (John 12:27) that You might be glorified when I am deeply humbled and am delivered through You. Let it be Your pleasure to deliver me, for what can I do who am poor, and without You where will I go? Give patience this time also. Help me, O Lord my God, and I will not fear no matter how much I am weighed down.

And now amid these things what shall I say? Lord, Your will be done. I have well deserved to be troubled and weighed down. Therefore I ought to bear patiently until the tempest is passed and comfort returns. Yet is Your omnipotent arm able also to take this temptation away from me and to lessen its power that I not fall utterly under it, even as You have helped me many times in the past, O my merciful God. And as difficult as this deliverance is for me, so easy is it for You, O right hand of the Most High.

CHAPTER 29

OF SEEKING DIVINE HELP

"My child, I the Lord am 'a stronghold in the day of trouble' (Nahum 1:7). Come to Me when it is not well with you.

"This is what mostly hinders heavenly consolation: that you are too slow to turn to Me in prayer. For before you earnestly seek Me, you first seek after many means of comfort, and refresh yourself in outward things. So it comes to pass that all things profit you but little until you learn that it is I who deliver those who trust in Me, and apart from Me there is no strong help or profitable counsel. But now, recovering courage after the tempest, you grow strong in the light of My mercies, for I am near, that I may restore all things not only as they were at the first, but also abundantly.

"For is anything too hard for Me, or will I be like one who does not keep his promises? Where is your faith? Stand fast and persevere. Be long-suffering and strong. Consolation will come to you in its due season. Wait for Me; I will come and heal you. It is temptation that vexes you and a vain fear that terrifies you. What does care about future events bring you except sorrow? 'Sufficient for the day is its own trouble' (Matthew 6:34). It is useless to be disturbed about future things that perhaps will never come.

"But it is the nature of man to be deceived by concerns of this sort, and it is a sign of a mind that is still weak to be so easily distracted by the suggestion of the enemy. For the enemy does not care whether he deceive and beguile by true means or false; whether he throw you down by the love of the present or fear of the future. Therefore 'let not your heart be troubled, neither let it be afraid' (John 14:27). Believe in Me, and put your trust in My mercy (Psalm 33:22). When you think you are far removed from Me, I am often the nearer. When you think that almost all is lost, then often is greater opportunity of gain at hand. All is not lost when something goes contrary to your wishes. You ought not judge according to present feeling.

"Think not yourself totally abandoned, although for the time I have sent you some trial, or have even withdrawn some cherished consolation; for this is the way to the kingdom of heaven. And without doubt it is better for you and for all My other servants that you should be proven by adversities than that you should have all things as you want. I know your hidden thoughts and that it is very important for your soul's health that sometimes you be left without pleasure, lest you be lifted up by prosperity and desire to please yourself in that which you are not. What I have given I am able to take away, and to restore again at My good pleasure.

"When I shall have given you something, it is Mine; when I shall have taken it away, I have not taken what is yours; for 'every good gift and every perfect gift is from Me' (James 1:17). If I shall have sent on you grief or irritation, do not be angry, nor let your heart be sad; I am able to quickly lift you up and change every burden into joy. But I am just and greatly to be praised when I do thus to you.

"If you rightly consider and look upon it with truth, you ought never to be so sadly cast down because of adversity, but rather should rejoice and give thanks; indeed, count it the highest joy that I afflict you with sorrows. 'As the Father loved Me, I also have loved you' (John 15:9). Thus have I spoken to My beloved disciples, whom I sent forth not to worldly joys but to great strivings; not to honors but to contempt; not to ease but to labors; not to rest but to bring forth much fruit with patience. My child, remember these words."

CHAPTER 30

OF THE CASTING AWAY
OF ALL SELFISHNESS

"My child, you cannot possess perfect liberty unless you completely deny yourself. All who are enslaved are possessors of riches, those who love themselves, the selfish, the curious, the restless; those who ever seek after soft things and not after the things of Jesus Christ; those who continually plan that which will not stand. For whatever comes not of God will perish. Hold fast the saying, 'Renounce all things, and you will find all things; give up your lust, and you will find rest.' Dwell on this in your mind, and you will understand all things."

O Lord, this is not the work of a day, nor children's play; truly in this short saying is enclosed all the perfection of the religious.

"My child, you ought not be discouraged because you have heard the way of the perfect. Rather ought you to be motivated to higher aims. Oh that you were not a lover of your self but were always focusing on Me. Then you would please Me greatly and your life would go on in joy and peace. You still have many things to renounce, which if you resign not utterly to Me, you will not gain what you seek. 'I counsel you to buy from Me gold refined in the fire, that you may be rich' (Revelation 3:18), that is, heavenly wisdom, which despises all base things. Put away from you earthly wisdom and all pleasure."

CHAPTER 31

OF DIRECTING THE
AIM TOWARD GOD

"My child, do not trust your feelings, for that which is now will be quickly changed into something else. As long as you live you are subject to change; one moment you are joyful, the next sad; now at peace, now anxious; now studious, now careless. But the wise person stands above these changeable things, not attentive to what he may feel in himself but focused on the much-desired end. For thus will he be able to remain unshaken, his eyes being steadfastly fixed on Me.

CHAPTER 32

THAT GOD IS SWEET
TO THE ONE WHO LOVES

God is mine, and all things are mine! What more happy thing can I desire? When You are present all things are pleasant; when You are absent, all things are wearisome. You make the heart to be at rest, give it deep peace and joy. You make it to think rightly in every matter, and in every matter to give You praise. Nothing can please long without You but if it would be pleasant, Your grace must be there, and it is Your wisdom that must give it a sweet savor.

To him who tastes You, what can be distasteful? And to him who tastes You not, what is there that can make him joyful? But the worldly wise and those who enjoy the flesh fail in Your wisdom; for in the wisdom of the world is found utter vanity, and to be carnally minded is death. But those who follow after You through contempt of worldly things and dying to the flesh are found to be the truly wise because they are carried from futility to truth, from the flesh to the spirit. They taste that the Lord is good, and whatever good they find in creatures, they count it all to the praise of the Creator. Very dissimilar is the enjoyment of the Creator compared to enjoyment of the creature, the enjoyment of eternity and of time, of light uncreated and of light reflected.

O Light everlasting, surpassing all created lights, dart down Your ray from on high that will pierce the innermost depths of my heart. Give purity, joy, clarity, life to my spirit, that with all its powers it may cling to You with rapture. Oh, when will that blessed and longed-for time come when You will satisfy me with Your presence and be to me all in all? So long as this is delayed, my joy will not be full. The old man still lives in me; he is not yet completely crucified, not yet quite dead; still he lusts fiercely against the spirit, wages inward wars, and does not allow the soul's kingdom to be at peace.

But You who rule the raging of the sea and still the waves when they arise (see Psalm 89:9), rise up and help me. "Scatter the peoples who delight in war" (Psalm 68:30). Destroy them by Your power. Show forth Your might, and let Your right hand be glorified, for I have no hope, no refuge, except in You, O Lord my God.

CHAPTER 33

THAT THERE IS NO SECURITY AGAINST TEMPTATION

"My child, you are never secure in this life, but you will need your spiritual armor as long as you live. You dwell among foes and are attacked on the right hand and on the left. If, therefore, you do not use the shield of patience on all sides, you will not remain long unwounded. Above all, if you do not keep your heart fixed on Me with steadfast purpose and bear all things for My sake, you will not be able to bear the fierceness of the attack or attain to the victory of the blessed. Therefore must you struggle bravely all your life and put forth a strong hand against those things that oppose you. For to him who overcomes is the hidden manna given (Revelation 2:17), but great misery is reserved for the slothful.

"If you seek rest in this life, how then will you attain to the rest that is eternal? Do not try to attain great rest but great patience. Seek true peace, not in earth but in heaven, not in man nor in any created thing, but in God alone. For the love of God you must willingly undergo all things, whether labors or sorrows, temptations, irritations, anxieties, needs, weakness, offenses, opposition, rebukes, humiliations, confusion, correction. These things develop virtue, these things prove the scholar of Christ, these things fashion the heavenly crown. I will give you an eternal reward for short labor, and infinite glory for temporary shame.

"Do you think that you will always have spiritual consolation whenever you want it? My saints never had that but instead suffered many griefs, temptations, and heavy desolations. But patiently they bore themselves throughout them all and trusted in God more than in themselves, knowing that 'the sufferings of this present time are not worthy to be compared with the glory which shall be revealed in us' (Romans 8:18). Do you think that you will obtain immediately what many have reached only after many tears and hard labors? Wait for the Lord and be strong; do not be faint-hearted, nor turn aside from Me, but constantly devote your body and soul to the glory of God. I will reward you generously, I will be with you in trouble (see Psalm 91:15)."

Chapter 34

Against Vain Judgments of Men

"My child, anchor your soul firmly in God and do not fear man's judgment when your conscience pronounces you innocent. It is good to suffer in this way, nor will it be grievous to the heart that is humble and trusts in God more than in itself. Many men have opinions, and therefore little trust is to be placed in them. Moreover, it is impossible to please all. Although Paul studied to please all men in the Lord and to 'become all things to all men' (1 Corinthians 9:22), yet nevertheless with him it was a very small thing to be judged by man (see 1 Corinthians 4:3).

"He labored abundantly, as much as he was able, for the building up and the salvation of others, but he could not avoid being sometimes judged and despised by others. Therefore he committed all to God, who knew all, and with patience and humility defended himself against evil speakers, foolish and false thinkers, and those who accused him. Nevertheless, from time to time he replied, lest his silence should become a stumbling block to those who were weak.

"Who are you, that you should be afraid of a man that shall die? Today he is here, and tomorrow his place is not found. Fear God and you will not tremble before the terrors of men. What can any man do against you by words or deeds? He hates himself more than you, nor will he escape the judgment of God. Keep God before your eyes, and do not contend with fretful words. And if for the present you seem to give way and to suffer confusion that you have not deserved, do not be angry at this, nor by impatience diminish your reward; but rather look to Me in heaven, for I am able to deliver you from all confusion and hurt and to give to every man according to his works."

CHAPTER 35

OF ENTIRE RESIGNATION
OF SELF

"My child, lose yourself and you will find Me. For more grace will be added to you as soon as you surrender yourself, and as long as you do not take yourself back again."

O Lord, how often do I need to surrender myself, and in what things should I lose myself?

"Always; every hour: in the little things and the big things. I make no exception but want you to be found stripped in all things. Otherwise how can you be Mine and I yours, unless you are free from every will of your own? The sooner you do this, the better will it be with you, and the more abundantly will you be rewarded.

"Some surrender themselves but with certain reservations, for they do not fully trust in God, therefore they think that they have some provision to make for themselves. Some again at first offer everything, but later, being tempted, they return to their own ways and thus make no progress in virtue. They will not attain to the true liberty of a pure heart, nor to the grace of My sweet companionship, unless they first entirely surrender themselves and daily offer themselves up as a sacrifice.

"Many times I have said to you, and now say again, 'Give yourself up, surrender yourself, and you will have great inward peace.' Give all for all; demand nothing, ask nothing in return; stand simply and with no hesitation in Me, and you will possess Me. You will have liberty of heart, and the darkness will not overwhelm you. Strive for this, pray for it, long after it, that you may be delivered from all possession of yourself and unreservedly follow Jesus, may die to yourself and live eternally for Me. Then will all vain thoughts disappear, all spiritual unrest, and superfluous cares. Then also will fear depart from you, and lust shall die."

CHAPTER 36

THAT PEOPLE MUST NOT BE IMMERSED IN BUSINESS

"My child, always commit your cause to Me; I will take care of it in the right way at the right time. Wait for My arrangement of it, and then you will find it working for your good."

O Lord, freely I commit all things to You, for my planning can profit but little. Oh, that I did not dwell so much on future events but could offer myself completely to Your pleasure without delay.

"My child, people often strive passionately after things they desire, but when they have obtained them they begin to change their mind about them, because their affections toward them are not lasting, but rather rush from one thing to another. Therefore it is not really a small thing when in small things we resist self."

The true progress of man lies in self-denial, and a man who denies himself is free and safe. But the old enemy, opposer of all good things, does not cease to tempt, but day and night sets his wicked snares to try to trap the unwary. "Watch and pray," says the Lord, "lest you enter into temptation" (Matthew 26:41).

CHAPTER 37

THAT MAN HAS NO GOOD IN HIMSELF

Lord, "what is man that You are mindful of him, and the son of man that You visit him?" (Psalm 8:4). What has man deserved, that You should bestow Your favor on him? Lord, what cause can I have of complaint, if You forsake me? Or what can I justly allege, if You refuse to hear my petition? This I may truly think and say, "Lord, I am nothing, I have nothing that is good of myself, but I fall short in all things. And unless I am helped by You and inwardly supported, I become altogether lukewarm and reckless."

But You, O Lord, are always the same and endure forever, always good, righteous, and holy, doing all things well and righteously. But I who am more ready to go forward than backward never continue in one place, because changes sevenfold pass over me. Yet it quickly becomes better when it so pleases You and You put forth Your hand to help me, because You alone can aid without the help of man and can so strengthen me that my countenance will be no more changed, but my heart will be turned to You and rest in You alone.

Wherefore, if I only knew well how to reject all human consolations, then could I worthily trust in Your grace and rejoice in the gift of Your consolation.

Thanks be to You whenever it goes well with me! But I am nothing in Your sight, fickle and weak. What then have I in which to glory, or why do I long to be held in honor? Is it not for nothing? This also is utterly meaningless. While a man pleases himself he displeases You; while he chases after the praises of man, he is deprived of true virtue.

But true glory and holy rejoicing lie in glorying in You and not in self; in rejoicing in Your name, not in our own virtue; in not taking delight in any creature, except only for Your sake. Let Your name, not mine, be praised; let Your work, not mine, be magnified; let Your holy name be blessed, but to me let nothing be given of the praises of men. You are my glory, You are the joy of my heart. In You will I make my boast and be glad all the day long, but for myself let me not glory "except in my infirmities" (2 Corinthians 12:5).

Truly all human glory, all temporal honor, all worldly exultation, compared to Your eternal glory, are meaningless. O God my Truth and my Mercy, to You alone be all praise, honor, power, and glory forever and ever. Amen.

CHAPTER 38

OF CONTEMPT FOR ALL TEMPORAL HONOR

"My child, do not let it bother you when you see others honored and exalted and yourself despised and humbled. Lift up your heart to Me in heaven, and then the contempt of men on earth will not make you sad."

O Lord, we are blind and quickly seduced by meaningless things. If I look rightly within myself, never was injury done to me by any creature, and therefore I have nothing about which to complain before You. But because I have many times grievously sinned against You, all creatures justly take up arms against me. Therefore to me confusion and contempt are justly due, but to You praise and honor and glory. And unless I am willing that every creature should despise and desert me and that I should be esteemed as nothing, I cannot be inwardly filled with peace and strength, nor spiritually enlightened, nor fully united to You.

CHAPTER 39

THAT OUR PEACE IS NOT TO BE PLACED IN PEOPLE

"My child, if you set your peace on any person because you have a high opinion of him and are familiar with him, you will be unstable. But if you seek the ever-living and abiding Truth, the desertion or death of a friend will not make you sad. In Me ought the love of your friend subsist, and for My sake is everyone to be loved who appears to you good and is very dear to you in this life. Without Me friendship has no strength or endurance, neither is that love true and pure that I do not unite. You ought to be so dead to such affections of beloved friends that as far as in you lies you would rather choose to be without any companionship. The nearer a man approaches to God, the further he recedes from all earthly comfort. The deeper also he descends into himself and the more sinful he appears in his own eyes, the higher he ascends toward God.

"But he who attributes anything good to himself hinders the grace of God from coming to him, because the grace of the Holy Spirit ever seeks the humble heart. If you could make yourself utterly nothing and empty yourself of the love of every creature, then would it be My part to fill you with great grace. When you set your eyes on creatures, the face of the Creator is withdrawn from you. Learn in all things to conquer yourself for your Creator's sake, then will you be able to attain divine knowledge. However small anything be, if it is loved and regarded excessively, it holds us back from the highest good and corrupts us.

CHAPTER 40

AGAINST MEANINGLESS WORLDLY KNOWLEDGE

"My child, do not let the words of men move you. 'For the kingdom of God is not in word but in power' (1 Corinthians 4:20). Listen to My words, for they kindle the heart and enlighten the mind, they bring contrition, and they supply much consolation. Never read the Word so that you may appear more knowledgeable or wise, but study for the mortification of your sins, for this will be far more profitable for you than the knowledge of many difficult questions.

"When you have read and learned many things, you must always return to one first principle. I am 'He who teaches man knowledge' (Psalm 94:10), and I give children clearer knowledge than can be taught by people. He to whom I speak will be quickly wise and will grow much in the spirit.

"I am He who in an instant lifts up the humble spirit to learn more of the eternal truth than if a man had studied ten years in school. I teach without noise of words, without confusion of opinions, without striving after honor, without clash of arguments. I am He who teaches men to despise earthly things, to loathe things present, to seek things heavenly, to enjoy things eternal, to flee honors, to endure offences, to place all hope in Me, to desire nothing apart from Me, and above all things to love Me fervently."

CHAPTER 41

OF NOT TROUBLING OURSELVES
ABOUT OUTWARD THINGS

"My child, in many things it is good for you to be ignorant and to consider yourself as one to whom the whole world is crucified. It is more profitable to turn away your eyes from those things that displease and to leave each man to his own opinion than to give yourself to debates that cause strife. If you stand well with God and have His judgment in your mind, you will easily bear to be as one conquered."

CHAPTER 42

THAT WE MUST NOT BELIEVE EVERYONE

Lord, "give us help from trouble, for the help of man is useless" (Psalm 60:11). How often have I failed to find faithfulness where I thought I possessed it. How many times I have found it where I least expected. Useless therefore is hope in people, but the salvation of the just, O God, is in You. You are blessed in all things that happen to us. We are weak and unstable, we are quickly deceived and easily changed.

Who is the man who is able to keep himself so carefully as to not sometimes come into some snare of perplexity? But he who trusts in You, O Lord, and seeks You with a sincere heart does not easily slip. And if he falls into any tribulation, however he may be entangled, yet very quickly he will be delivered by You, or by You will be comforted, because You will not forsake him who trusts in You to the end. A friend who continues faithful in all the distresses of his friend is rare to be found. You alone, O Lord, are most faithful in all things, and there is no one else like You.

With what wisdom have You warned us to

"beware of men," and that "a man's enemies will be those of his own household" (Matthew 10:17, 36). I have been taught by my loss and desire that I may prove to be more careful and not foolish. Protect me, O Lord, from mischievous and reckless men; do not let me fall into their hands. Put a true and steadfast word in my mouth and remove a deceitful tongue from me. What I do not want to suffer I ought by all means to avoid doing.

Oh, how good a thing it is to be silent concerning others and not to carelessly believe all reports or spread them further; how good also to lay one's self open to few, to seek ever to have You as the beholder of the heart; to not be carried about with every wind of words, but to desire that all things be done according to the good pleasure of Your will! How safe for the preserving of heavenly grace to flee from human approval and not to long after the things that seem to win admiration abroad, but to follow with all earnestness those things that bring improvement of life and heavenly fervor! How many have been harmed by their virtue being made known and too hastily praised. How truly profitable has grace been preserved in silence in this frail life, which, as we are told, is all temptation and warfare.

CHAPTER 43

WHEN EVIL WORDS ARE THROWN AT US

"My child, stand fast and believe in Me. For what are words but merely words? They fly through the air, but they bruise no stone. If you are guilty, think how you would gladly amend yourself; if you know nothing against yourself, consider that you will gladly bear this for God's sake. It is little enough that you sometimes have to bear hard words, for you are not yet able to bear hard blows. And why do such trivial matters go to your heart, except that you are yet carnal and regard men more than you ought? For because you fear to be despised, you are unwilling to be reproved for your faults and make paltry excuses.

"But look better into yourself, and you will know that the world is still alive in you and the futile love of pleasing men. For when you refuse to be humbled by your faults, it is plain that you are neither truly humble nor truly dead to the world, and that the world is not crucified to you. But listen to My Word, and you will not care for ten thousand words of men. If all things could be said against you that the utmost malice could invent, how would it hurt you if you were to let it go and make no more account of it than a particle of dust? Could it pluck out a single hair of your head?

"But he who has no heart within him and does not have God before his eyes is easily moved by a word of reproach; but he who trusts in Me and does not seek to abide by his own judgment will be free from the fear of men. For I am the judge and the discerner of all secrets; I know how the thing has been done; I know both the injurer and the bearer. From Me went forth that Word, by My permission this has happened, 'that the thoughts of many hearts may be revealed' (Luke 2:35). I will judge the guilty and the innocent, but beforehand I have willed to try them both by a secret judgment.

"The testimony of men often deceives. My judgment is true; it will stand, and it will not be overturned. It commonly lies hidden and only to a few in certain cases is it made known; yet it never errs, nor can err, although it does not seem right to the eyes of foolish men. To Me, therefore, must people turn and not lean on their own opinion. For 'no grave trouble will overtake the righteous' (Proverbs 12:21), whatever may be sent to him by God. Even if an unjust charge is brought against him, he will care little, and if through others he is vindicated he will not exult above measure. For he considers that I am He who 'tests the hearts and minds' (Psalm 7:9), who does not judge according to outward appearance."

O Judge, just, strong, and patient, who knows the frailty and sinfulness of men, be my strength and confidence, for my own conscience is not sufficient. You know what I do not know, and therefore ought I under all rebuke to humble myself and bear it meekly. Therefore mercifully forgive me as often as I have not done this, and grant me the next time the grace of greater endurance. For better to me is Your abundant pity for the attainment of Your pardon than the righteousness that I believe myself to have for defence against my conscience. Although "I know of nothing against myself, yet I am not justified by this" (1 Corinthians 4:4), because if Your mercy were removed, in Your sight no one living would be justified (see Psalm 143:2).

CHAPTER 44

THAT ALL TROUBLES ARE TO BE ENDURED FOR THE SAKE OF ETERNAL LIFE

"My child, do not let the labors you have undertaken for Me wear you down, nor let trials discourage you in any way, but let My promise strengthen and comfort you in every event. I am sufficient to reward you above all measure. Not long will you labor here, nor always be weighed down with sorrows. Wait a little while, and you will see a speedy end to your troubles. An hour will come when all labor and confusion will cease.

"Earnestly do whatever you do; labor faithfully in My vineyard. I will be your reward. Write, read, sing, weep, be silent, pray, endure adversities courageously; eternal life is worthy of all these conflicts, indeed, and of greater. Peace shall come in 'one day which is known to the Lord—neither day nor night' (Zechariah 14:7), and light eternal, infinite clarity, steadfast peace, and undisturbed rest. You will not say then, 'Who will deliver me from this body of death?' (Romans 7:24), because death will be utterly destroyed, and there will be salvation that can never fail, no more anxiety, happy delight, sweet and noble society.

"Oh, if you saw the unfading crowns of the saints in heaven and with what great glory they now rejoice, who before were considered by this world contemptible and unworthy of life, truly you would immediately humble yourself and would desire rather to be in subjection to all than to have authority over one; nor would you long for pleasant days in this life but would rejoice to be afflicted for God's sake and consider it gain to be counted nothing among men.

"Oh, if these things were sweet to your taste and moved you to the bottom of your heart, how would you dare even once to complain? Are not all difficult things to be endured for the sake of eternal life? It is no small thing, the losing or gaining of the kingdom of God. Lift up therefore your face to heaven. Behold, I and all My saints with Me now rejoice, are now comforted, are now secure, are now at peace, and will remain with Me forever in the kingdom of My Father."

CHAPTER 45

OF THE DAY OF ETERNITY

Oh, most blessed mansion of the city above! Oh, most clear day of eternity that the night does not obscure, but the supreme truth ever enlightens! Day always joyful, always secure, and never changing its state into those that are contrary. Oh, that this day might shine forth, and that all these temporal things would come to an end. It shines indeed upon the saints, glowing with unending brightness, but only from afar and through a glass, upon those who are pilgrims on the earth.

The citizens of heaven know how glorious that day is; the exiled sons of Eve groan, because this is bitter and wearisome. The days of life are few, full of sorrows and hardships, where man is defiled with many sins, ensnared with many passions, bound fast with many fears, wearied with many cares, distracted with many questions, entangled with many meaningless pursuits, surrounded by many errors, worn away with many labors, weighed down with temptations, weakened by pleasures, tormented by poverty.

When will there be an end to these evils? When will I be delivered from the wretched slavery of my sins? When will I be mindful, O

Lord, of You alone? When will I rejoice in You to the fullest? When will I be in true liberty without any hindrance, without any burden on mind or body? When will there be solid peace, peace within and without, peace firm on every side? Blessed Jesus, when will I stand to behold You? When will I gaze on the glory of Your kingdom? When will You be to me all in all? When will I be with You in Your kingdom that You have prepared from the foundation of the world for those who love You?

Relieve my sorrow, for toward You all my desire longs. For whatever this world offers me for consolation is a burden. I yearn to enjoy You intimately, but I cannot attain it. I long to cling to heavenly things, but temporal things and unmortified passions press me down. In my mind I would be above all things, but in my flesh I am unwillingly compelled to be beneath them. So wretched man that I am, I fight with myself and am made grievous even to myself, while the spirit seeks to be above and the flesh to be beneath.

How I suffer inwardly when I am thinking about heavenly things and presently a crowd of carnal things rushes upon me. My God, do not be far from me, nor depart in wrath from Your servant. Let all delusions of my enemy be confounded. Recall my senses to Yourself, cause me to forget all worldly things; help me to quickly cast away and despise the imaginations of sin. Help me, eternal Truth, that no vanity may move me. Come to me, O heavenly Sweetness, and let all impurity flee from before Your face. Pardon me also, and in Your mercy deal gently with me, whenever in prayer I think on anything besides You; for truly I confess that I am easily distracted. Where my thoughts are, there am I; and there commonly is my thought where that which I love is. That which naturally delights readily occurs to me.

You have plainly said, "Where your treasure is, there your heart will be also" (Matthew 6:21). If I love heaven, I gladly meditate on heavenly things. If I love the world, I rejoice in the delights of the world and am made sorry by its adversities. If I love the flesh, I am continually imagining the things that belong to the flesh; if I love the spirit, I am delighted by meditating on spiritual things. For whatever things I love, about these I readily converse and carry home with me their images. But blessed is that man who for Your sake is willing to part from all creatures and who crucifies the lusts of the flesh by the fervor of his spirit, so that with serene conscience he may offer to You a pure prayer, having shut out from himself all worldly things.

CHAPTER 46

OF THE DESIRE AFTER ETERNAL LIFE

"My child, when you feel the desire for eternal happiness to be poured into you from above and long to depart from the tabernacle of this body that you may contemplate My unchangeable glory, enlarge your heart and take in this holy inspiration with all your desire. Give most hearty thanks to the Supreme Goodness, who deals with you so graciously, visits you so lovingly, stirs you up so fervently, raises you so powerfully, lest you sink down to earthly things. For not by your own meditating or striving do you receive this gift, but by the sole gracious condescension of supreme grace and divine regard, that you may make progress in virtue, prepare yourself for future conflicts, cling to Me with all the affection of your heart, and strive to serve Me with fervent will.

"My child, often the fire burns, but the flame ascends not without smoke. So also the desires of some men burn toward heavenly things, and yet they are not free from the temptation of carnal affection. Thus therefore they are not acting with an altogether simple desire for God's glory when they pray to Him so earnestly. Such, too, is often your desire, when you have imagined it to be so earnest. For that which is tainted with your own self-seeking is not pure and perfect.

"Do not seek what is pleasant and advantageous to yourself but what is acceptable and honorable to Me; for if you judge rightly, you must choose and follow after My will rather than your own desire, indeed, rather than anything that can be desired. I know your desire, and I have heard your many groanings. Already you long to be in the glorious liberty of the children of God; already the eternal home delights you. But the hour is not yet come; there remains still another season, even a season of warfare, a season of labor and trial. You desire to be filled with the Chief Good, but you cannot attain it immediately. I am that good; wait for Me, until the kingdom of God comes.

"You must still be tried on earth and be exercised in many things. Consolation will from time to time be given you, but abundant satisfaction will not be granted. Be strong therefore, and be brave in both working and suffering things that are against your nature. You must put on the new man and be changed into another man. You must often do what you do not want to do, and you must leave undone what you want to do. What pleases others will have good success, what pleases you will not prosper. What others say will be listened to; what you say will not be heard. Others will ask and receive; you will ask and not obtain. Others will be great in the report of men, but about you will nothing be spoken. To others this or that will be entrusted; you will be considered useful for nothing.

"For this reason nature will sometimes be filled with sadness, and it is a great thing if you bear it silently. In this and many similar things the faithful servant of the Lord is going to be tried, how far he is able to deny himself and bring himself into subjection in all things. Scarcely is there anything in which you have need to mortify yourself so much as in seeing things that are adverse to your will, especially when things are commanded you to be done that seem to you inexpedient or of little use to you. And because you dare not resist a higher power, being under authority, therefore it seems hard for you to shape your course according to the nod of another and to forego your own opinion.

"But consider, My child, the fruit of these labors, the swift end, and the great reward, and you will find it no pain to bear them but rather that they are the strongest solace. For even in exchange for this trifling desire that you have readily forsaken, you will always have your will in heaven. There truly you will find all that you desire, all that you can long for. There you will have all good within your power without the fear of losing it. There your will, ever at one with Mine, will desire nothing outward, nothing for itself. There no man will withstand you, none will complain of you, none will hinder, nothing will stand in your path; but all things desired by you will be present together and will refresh your whole affection and fill it up to the brim. There I will glory for the scorn suffered here, the garment of praise for sorrow, and for the lowest place a throne in the kingdom forever. There will appear the fruit of obedience, the labor of repentance will rejoice, and humble subjection will be crowned gloriously."

CHAPTER 47

HOW A DESOLATE MAN OUGHT TO COMMIT HIMSELF INTO THE HANDS OF GOD

O Lord, be blessed now and forevermore; because as You will, so it is done, and what You do is good. Let Your servant rejoice in You, not in himself, nor in any other; because You alone are my true joy, my hope and my crown, my joy and my honor. What does Your servant have that he received not from You, without merit of his own? You are all things that You have given and that You have made. "I have been afflicted and ready to die from my youth" (Psalm 88:15), and my soul is sorrowful, sometimes also it is disturbed within itself, because of the sufferings that are coming on it.

I long for the joy of peace; for the peace of Your children do I pray, for in the light of Your comfort they are fed by You. If You give peace, if You pour into me holy joy, the soul of Your servant will be full of melody and devout in Your praise. But if You withdraw Yourself, as too often You are accustomed, he will not be able to run in the way of Your commandments, but rather he will strike his breast and bow his knees, because it is not with him as it was yesterday and the day before, when Your lamp shone on my head (see Job 29:3) and he hid under the shadow of Your wings (see Psalm 17:8).

O Father, righteous and ever to be praised, the hour comes when Your servant is to be proved. O beloved Father, it is well that in this hour Your servant suffer something for Your sake. O Father, ever to be adored, the hour comes that You foreknew from everlasting, when for a little while Your servant should outwardly bow down but always live inwardly with You; when for a little while he should be little regarded, humbled, and fail in the eyes of men; should be wasted with sufferings and weaknesses, to rise again with You in the dawn of the new light and be glorified in the heavenly places. You have ordained it so, and so have willed it; and that which You Yourself have commanded is done.

For this is Your favor to Your friend, that he should suffer and be troubled in the world for Your love's sake, however often, and by whomever You have allowed it to be done. Without Your counsel and providence, and without cause, nothing comes to pass on the earth. "It is good for me that I have been afflicted, that I may learn Your statutes" (Psalm 119:71), and may cast away all pride of heart and presumption. It is good for me that confusion has covered my face, that I may seek You for consolation rather than men. By this also I have learned to dread Your unsearchable judgment, who afflicts the just with the wicked but not without equity and justice.

Thanks be to You, because You have not spared my sins but have beaten me with stripes of love, inflicting pain and sending troubles on me without and within. There is no one who can console me, but You only, O Lord my God, heavenly Physician of souls, who scourges and has mercy, who leads down to hell and brings up again. Your discipline over me and Your rod itself will teach me.

Beloved Father, I am in Your hands, I bow myself under the rod of Your correction. Smite my back and my neck that I may bend my crookedness to Your will. Make me a virtuous and lowly disciple, as You were accustomed to be kind, that I may walk according to every nod of Yours. To You I commend myself and all that I have for correction; better is it to be punished here than hereafter. You know all things, and nothing remains hidden from You in man's conscience. Before they are, You know that they will be, and You need not that any man teach You or admonish You concerning the things that are done on earth. You know what is good for me and how greatly trouble contributes to the scrubbing off of the rust of sin. Do with me according to Your desired good pleasure, and despise not my life that is full of sin, known to no one so entirely and fully as You.

Grant me, O Lord, to know that which ought to be known; to love that which ought to be loved; to praise that which pleases You most, to esteem that which is precious in Your sight, to reject that which is vile in Your eyes. Allow me not to judge according to my physical sight, nor to give sentence according to the hearing of the ears of ignorant people, but to discern in true judgment between visible and spiritual things, and above all things to be ever seeking after the will of Your good pleasure.

Often the senses of men are deceived in judging; the lovers of the world also are deceived in that they love only visible things. How is a man better because by man he is reckoned very great? The deceiver deceives the deceiver, the vain man the vain, the blind man the blind, the weak man the weak, when they exalt one another; and in truth they put to shame while they foolishly praise.

CHAPTER 48

THAT WE MUST GIVE OURSELVES TO HUMBLE WORKS

"My child, you are not able to live in a constant state of fervent desire for virtue, nor to stand fast in the loftier region of contemplation; but you must sometimes descend to lower things and bear the burden of corruptible life, though unwillingly and with weariness. As long as you wear a mortal body, you will feel weariness and heaviness of heart. Therefore you ought to groan often in the flesh because of the burden of the flesh, inasmuch as you cannot give yourself to spiritual studies and divine contemplation unceasingly.

"At such a time it is expedient for you to flee to humble, physical work and to renew yourself with good actions; to wait for My coming and heavenly visitation with confidence; to bear your exile and spiritual dryness with patience, until you are visited by Me again and freed from all anxieties. For I will cause you to forget your labors and to enjoy eternal peace. I will spread open before you the pleasant pastures of the scriptures, that with enlarged heart you may begin to run in the way of My commandments. And you will say, 'The sufferings of this present time are not worthy to be compared with the glory which shall be revealed in us' (Romans 8:18)."

CHAPTER 49

THAT A PERSON OUGHT NOT RECKON HIMSELF WORTHY OF CONSOLATION

O Lord, I am not worthy of Your consolation, nor of any spiritual visitation, therefore You deal justly with me when You leave me poor and desolate. For if I were able to pour forth tears like the sea, I would still not be worthy of Your consolation. Therefore am I worthy of nothing except to be scourged and punished, because I have grievously offended You many times and in many things have greatly sinned. Therefore, I am not worthy of even the least of Your consolations. But You, gracious and merciful God, who wills not that Your works should perish to show forth the riches of Your mercy on the vessels of mercy (Romans 9:23), stoop to comfort Your servant even beyond all his own deserving.

What have I done, O Lord, that You should bestow any heavenly comfort on me? I remember not that I have done any good but have been ever prone to sin and slow to improve. It is true and I cannot deny it. If I should say otherwise, You would rise up against me and there would be no one to defend me. What have I deserved for my sins but hell and everlasting fire? I confess that I am worthy of all scorn and contempt, nor is it appropriate that I should be remembered among Your faithful servants. And although I am unwilling to hear this, nevertheless I will, for the truth's sake, accuse myself of my sins, that the more readily I may be accounted worthy of Your mercy.

What shall I say, guilty that I am and filled with confusion? I have no words to utter, unless it be this word alone, "I have sinned, Lord; have mercy on me, forgive me." "Leave me alone, that I may take a little comfort, before I go to the place from which I shall not return, to the land of darkness and the shadow of death" (Job 10:20–21). What do You require of a guilty and miserable sinner but that he be contrite and humble himself for his sins? In true contrition and humility of heart is birthed the hope of pardon, the troubled conscience is reconciled, lost grace is recovered, a person is preserved from the wrath to come, and God and the penitent hasten to meet each other with a holy kiss (see Luke 15:20).

The humble contrition of sinners is an acceptable sacrifice to You, O Lord, sending forth a smell sweeter to You by far than incense. This also is that pleasant ointment that You would have poured on Your sacred feet, "a broken and a contrite heart—these, O God, You will not despise" (Psalm 51:17). There is the place of refuge from the angry countenance of the enemy. There is washed away whatever evil has been contracted.

CHAPTER 50

THAT THE GRACE OF GOD DOES NOT JOIN WITH THOSE WHO MIND EARTHLY THINGS

"My child, precious is My grace. It does not allow itself to be joined with outward things, nor with earthly consolations. Therefore you ought to cast away all things that hinder grace, if you long to receive the inpouring thereof. Seek a secret place for yourself, love to dwell alone with yourself, desire the conversation of no one; but rather pour out your devout prayer to God, that you may possess a contrite mind and a pure conscience. Count the whole world as nothing; seek to be alone with God before all outward things. For you cannot be alone with Me and at the same time be delighted with transitory things. You ought to be separated from your acquaintances and dear friends, and keep your mind free from all worldly comfort.

"Oh, what great confidence will there be for the dying man whom no affection for anything detains in the world! But to have a heart so separated from all things, a sickly soul does not yet comprehend, nor does a carnal person know the liberty of a spiritual person. But if indeed he desires to be spiritually minded, he must renounce both those who are far off and those who are near, and to beware of no man more than himself. If you perfectly conquer yourself, very easily will you subdue all things besides. Perfect victory is triumph over oneself. For whoever keeps himself in subjection, in such a way that the sensual affections obey the reason and the reason in all things obeys Me, he truly is conqueror of himself.

"If you desire to climb to this height, you ought to start bravely and to lay the axe to the root, in order that you may pull up and destroy the hidden, excessive inclination toward yourself and toward all selfish and earthly good. From the sin of loving oneself too much almost everything hangs that needs to be utterly overcome. When that evil is conquered and put under foot, there will be great peace and tranquility continually. But because few strive earnestly to die perfectly to themselves, therefore do they remain entangled in themselves and cannot be raised in spirit above themselves. But he who desires to walk at liberty with Me must mortify all his passions and must cling to no creature with selfish love."

CHAPTER 51

OF THE DIVERSE WORKINGS
OF NATURE AND GRACE

"My child, pay diligent heed to the workings of nature and grace, because they move in a very different manner and are hardly distinguished except by a spiritual enlightened person. Everyone seeks good and makes pretense of something good in all that they say or do; and thus under the appearance of good many are deceived.

"Nature is deceitful and draws away, ensnares, and deceives many, and always has self for her end; but grace walks in simplicity and turns away from every appearance of evil, makes no false pretenses, and does all entirely for the sake of God.

"Nature is very unwilling to die, to be pressed down, to be overcome, to be in subjection, and to bear the yoke readily; but grace studies self-mortification, resists sensuality, seeks to be subdued, longs to be conquered, and wills not to use her own liberty. She loves to be held by discipline and not to have authority over any, but always to have her being under God, and for God's sake is ready to be humbly subject to every ordinance of man.

"Nature labors for her own advantage and considers what profit she may gain from another; but grace considers more, not what may be useful and convenient to self, but what may be profitable to many.

"Nature willingly receives honor and reverence; but grace faithfully ascribes all honor and glory to God.

"Nature fears confusion and contempt, but grace rejoices to suffer shame for the name of Jesus.

"Nature loves ease and bodily rest; grace cannot be idle but gladly embraces labor.

"Nature seeks to possess things interesting and attractive, and abhors those that are rough and cheap; grace is delighted with things simple and humble, despises not those that are rough, nor refuses to be clothed with old garments.

"Nature has regard for temporal things, rejoices in money, is made sad by loss, is vexed by any little hurtful word; but grace reaches after things eternal, clings not to those that are temporal, is not perturbed by losses or embittered by hard words, because she has placed her treasure and joy in heaven where nothing perishes.

"Nature is covetous and receives more willingly than she gives, loves things that are personal and private to herself; while grace is kind and generous, avoids selfishness, is contented with a little, believes that it is more blessed to give than to receive.

"Nature inclines you to created things, to your own flesh, to vanities and dissipation; but grace draws to God and to virtues, renounces creatures, flees from the world, and hates the desires of the flesh.

"Nature is glad to receive some outward solace in which the senses may have delight; but grace seeks to be comforted in God alone.

"Nature does everything for her own gain and profit, can do nothing as a free favor but hopes to attain something as good or better, or some praise or favor for her benefits, and she loves that her own deeds and gifts should be highly valued; but grace seeks nothing temporal, nor requires any other gift of reward than God alone; neither does she long for more of temporal necessities than what suffices for the attaining of eternal life.

"Nature rejoices in many friends and family, she boasts of noble place and noble birth, she smiles on the powerful, flatters the rich, applauds those who are like herself; but grace loves even her enemies and is not made proud by a multitude of friends, puts no store on high place or high birth, unless there be greater virtue therewith; favors the poor man more than the rich, has more sympathy with the innocent than with the powerful; rejoices with the truthful, not with the liar; always exhorts the good to strive after better gifts of grace and to become more like the Son of God.

"Nature quickly complains of poverty and trouble; grace bears want with constancy.

"Nature looks on all things in reference to herself, strives and argues for self; but grace brings back all things to God from whom they came at the beginning; ascribes no good to herself nor arrogantly presumes; is not contentious, nor prefers her own opinion to others, but in every sense and understanding submits herself to the eternal wisdom and the divine judgment.

"Nature is eager to know secrets and hear new things; she desires to be acknowledged and to do things that win praise and admiration. But grace does not care to hear new or interesting tidbits, because all this springs from the old corruption. So she works to restrain the senses, to shun futile complacency and ostentation, to humbly hide those things that deserve praise and admiration, and from everything and in all knowledge to seek after useful fruit and the praise and honor of

God. She desires not to receive praise for herself or her own but longs that God be blessed in all His gifts, who out of pure love bestows all things."

This grace is a supernatural light and a special gift of God, the proper mark of the elect, and the pledge of eternal salvation; it exalts a man from earthly things to love those that are heavenly; and it makes the carnal man spiritual. So far therefore as nature is utterly pressed down and overcome, so far is greater grace bestowed and the inner man is daily created anew after the image of God.

CHAPTER 52

OF THE CORRUPTION OF NATURE AND THE EFFECTIVENESS OF DIVINE GRACE

O Lord my God, grant me this grace, which You have shown to be so great and so necessary for salvation, that I may conquer my wicked nature, which draws me to sin and condemnation. For I feel in my flesh the law of sin, contradicting the law of my mind and bringing me into captivity to the obedience of sensuality in many things; nor can I resist its passions, unless Your grace enables me.

There is need of a great measure of Your grace, that my nature may be conquered, which has always been prone to evil.

O my God, I delight in Your law "according to the inward man" (Romans 7:22), knowing that Your "commandment [is] holy and just and good" (Romans 7:12); reproving also all evil and the sin that is to be avoided. Yet "with the flesh [I serve] the law of sin" (Romans 7:25), while I obey sensuality rather than reason. For this reason "to will [to do good] is present with me, but how to perform what is good I do not find" (Romans 7:18). So I often purpose many good things, but because grace is lacking to help my weakness, I fall backward in the face of a little resistance and fail. For that reason it comes to pass that I recognize the way of perfectness and see very clearly what things I ought to do; but pressed down by the weight of my own corruption, I do not rise to the things that are more perfect.

Oh, how entirely necessary is Your grace to me, O Lord, for a good beginning, for progress, and for bringing to perfection. For without it I can do nothing, but "I can do all things through Christ who strengthens me" (Philippians 4:13). Arts, riches, beauty, strength, wit, eloquence— they all have no use before You, O Lord, without Your grace. For the gifts of nature belong to good and evil alike; but the proper gift of the elect is grace—that is, love—and those who bear the mark of it are considered worthy of everlasting life. So mighty is this grace that without it neither the gift of prophecy nor the working of miracles, nor any speculation, however lofty, is of any value at all. But neither faith, nor hope, nor any other virtue is acceptable to You without love and grace.

O most blessed grace that makes the poor in spirit rich in virtues and renders him who is rich in many things humble in spirit, descend on me, fill me early with Your consolation, lest my soul fail through weariness and dryness of mind. I beseech You, O Lord, that I may find grace in Your sight, for Your grace is sufficient for me (see 2 Corinthians 12:9) when I do not obtain those things nature longs for. If I be tempted and tried by many trials, I will fear no evil as long as Your grace remains with me. This alone is my strength, this brings me counsel and help. It is more powerful than all enemies and wiser than all the wise men in the world.

It is the teacher of discipline, the light of the heart, the solace of anxiety, the banisher of sorrow, the deliverer from fear, the nurse of devotion, the drawer forth of tears. What am I without it but a dry tree, a useless branch, worthy to be cast away! Let your grace, therefore, O Lord, always keep and follow me and cause me to be continually given to all good works, through Jesus Christ, Your Son. Amen.

CHAPTER 53

THAT WE OUGHT TO DENY OURSELVES AND IMITATE CHRIST

"My child, so far as you are able to get outside of yourself so far will you be able to enter into Me. As for desire, no outward thing gives inner peace, so the forsaking of self inwardly joins your soul to God. I want you to learn perfect self-denial, living in My will without contradiction or complaint. Follow Me: 'I am the way, the truth, and the life' (John 14:6). I am the Way you ought to follow; the Truth you ought to believe; the Life you ought to hope for. I am the Way unchangeable; the Truth infallible; the Life everlasting. I am the Way altogether straight, the Truth supreme, the true Life, the blessed Life. If you remain in My way you will know the Truth, and 'the truth shall make you free' (John 8:32) and you will lay hold of eternal life.

"'If you want to enter into life, keep the commandments' (Matthew 19:17). If you will know the truth, believe in Me. 'If you want to be perfect, go, sell what you have' (Matthew 19:21). If you want to be My disciple, deny yourself. If you desire to possess the blessed life, despise the life that now is. If you want to be exalted in heaven, humble yourself in the world. If you want to reign with Me, bear the cross with Me; for only the servants of the cross find the way of blessedness and true light."

O Lord Jesus, inasmuch as Your life was difficult and despised by the world, help me to imitate You in despising the world, for "a disciple is not above his teacher, nor a servant above his master" (Matthew 10:24). Let Your servant walk in Your footsteps, because that is where my salvation and true holiness lay.

"My child, because you know these things and have read them all, you will be blessed if you do them. 'He who has My commandments and keeps them, it is he who loves Me. And he who loves Me will be loved by My Father, and I will love him and manifest Myself to him' (John 14:21), and I will make him to sit down with Me in My Father's kingdom."

O Lord Jesus, as You have said and promised, even so let it be to me and grant me to be proven worthy. I have received the cross at Your hand; I have carried it and will carry it even to death, as You have laid it on me. Truly the life of a devoted servant is a cross, but it leads to paradise. I have begun; I cannot turn back nor leave it.

Come, my friends, let us together go forward. Jesus will be with us. For Jesus' sake have we taken up this cross, for Jesus' sake let us persevere in the cross. He will be our helper, who was our captain and forerunner. Our King enters before us, and He will fight for us. Let us follow bravely. Let no one fear terrors; let us be prepared to die bravely in battle.

CHAPTER 54

THAT A PERSON MUST NOT BE TOO DISCOURAGED WHEN HE FALLS INTO SIN

"My child, patience and humility in adversities are more pleasing to Me than much comfort and devotion in prosperity. Why does a little thing spoken against you make you sad? And if it had been worse, you still should not be moved. But now allow it to pass; it is not the first and it will not be the last, if you live long. You are brave enough as long as no adversity meets you. You give good counsel also and know how to strengthen others with your words; but when tribulation suddenly knocks at your own door, your counsel and strength fail. Consider your great frailty, which you so often experience in trifling matters. Nevertheless, for your soul's health these things are done when they and other similar things happen to you.

"Put them away from your heart as well as you can, and if trials have touched you, do not let them discourage or entangle you long. At the least, bear them patiently, if you cannot bear them joyfully. And although you are very unwilling to hear it and feel vindication, check yourself and allow no unadvised word to come from your lips that might offend a weaker brother or sister. Soon the storm will be stilled and inner grief will be sweetened by returning grace. I yet live, says the Lord, ready to help you and to give you more than customary consolation if you put your trust in Me and devoutly call upon Me."

O Lord, Your Word is blessed, sweeter to my mouth than honey and the honeycomb. What would I do in the midst of my great tribulations and anxieties if You did not comfort me with Your holy words? As long as I am going to reach the haven of salvation, what does it matter what things I suffer or how many? Give me a good end, give me a happy passage out of this world. Remember me, O my God, and lead me by the right way to Your kingdom. Amen.

CHAPTER 55

OF DEEPER MATTERS

"My child, beware that you not dispute about high matters and the hidden judgments of God: why this person is thus left and that person is taken into such great favor; why this man is so greatly afflicted and that one so highly exalted. These things are beyond man's power to judge, neither does any reasoning have power to search out the divine judgments. When therefore the enemy suggests these things to you or when any curious people ask such questions, answer with this word of King David, 'Righteous are You, O Lord, and upright are Your judgments' (Psalm 119:137), and with this: 'The judgments of the Lord are true and righteous altogether' (Psalm 19:9). My judgments are to be feared, not disputed about, because they are incomprehensible to human understanding.

"I acknowledge the first and the last; I embrace all with inestimable love. I am to be praised in all My saints; I am to be blessed above all things and to be honored in everyone whom I have gloriously exalted and predestined, without any merit of their own. He who speaks against any of My saints speaks against Me and against all others in the kingdom of heaven.

"Be careful, My child, that you not have too much curiousity about those things that surpass your knowledge, but rather make this your business and give attention to it: seek to be found, even though it be the least, in the kingdom of God. Even if anyone could know who was holiest or who was considered greatest in the kingdom of heaven, what good would that knowledge do him, unless as a result of his knowledge he should humble himself all the more before Me and rise up to give greater praise to My name? He who considers how great his own sins are, how small his virtues, and how far removed he is from the perfection of the saints is far more acceptable in the sight of God than he who disputes about their greatness or littleness.

"Many ask who is greatest in the kingdom of heaven, not knowing whether they will be worthy to be counted among the least. It is a great thing to be even the least in heaven, where all are great, because all will be called and will be the sons of God. 'A little one shall become a thousand' (Isaiah 60:22), 'but the sinner being one hundred years old shall be accursed' (Isaiah 65:20). For when the disciples asked who should be the greatest in the kingdom of heaven, they received no other answer than this, 'Unless you are converted and become as little children, you will by no means enter the kingdom of heaven. Therefore whoever humbles himself as this little child is the greatest in the kingdom of heaven' (Matthew 18:3–4)."

What sorrow awaits those who disdain to humble themselves willingly with the little children, for the low gate of the kingdom of heaven will not allow them to enter in. What sorrow also awaits those who are rich, who have their consolation here (Philippians 2:21); because while the poor enter into the kingdom of God, they will stand outside lamenting. Rejoice, you humble, and exult, you poor, for yours is the kingdom of God if only you walk in the truth.

Chapter 56

That All Hope and Trust Are to Be Fixed in God Alone

O Lord, what is my trust in this life, and what is my greatest comfort? Is it not You, O Lord my God, whose mercies are without number? Where has it been well with me apart from You? Or what could be bad while You are near? I would rather be poor for Your sake than rich without You. I choose rather to be a pilgrim on the earth with You than to possess heaven without You. Where You are, there is heaven; and where You are not, there are death and hell. You are my desire, and therefore must I groan and cry and earnestly pray after You. In short, I can confide fully in no one to give me help in need but in You alone, O my God. You are my hope, You are my trust, You are my Comforter, and most faithful in all things.

You set forward only my salvation and turn all things for my good. Even though You expose me to various temptations and adversities, You ordain them all to my advantage, for You are accustomed to prove Your beloved ones in a thousand ways. In this proving You ought to be loved and praised no less than if You were filling me full of heavenly consolations.

In You, therefore, O Lord God, I put all my hope and my trust; on You I lay all my trouble and anguish, because I find people to be weak and unstable. For many friends will not profit, nor strong helpers be able to help, nor prudent counselors to give a useful answer, nor the books of the learned to console, nor any precious substance to deliver, nor any secret and beautiful place to give shelter, if You Yourself do not help, strengthen, comfort, instruct, keep in safety.

For all things that seem to belong to the attainment of peace and happiness are nothing when You are absent and bring no happiness at all in reality. Therefore are You the end of all good and the fullness of life and the soul of eloquence; and to hope in You above all things is the greatest comfort of Your servants. "My eyes are upon You" (Psalm 141:8); in You is my trust, O my God, Father of mercies.

According to the greatness of Your goodness and the multitude of Your mercies look upon me, and hear the prayer of Your poor servant. Protect and preserve the soul of the least of Your servants amid so many dangers in this corruptible life, and by Your grace direct it in the way of peace to its home of perpetual light. Amen.

Look for All of the FAITH CLASSICS from Barbour Publishing

Barbour's Faith Classics offer compelling, updated text and an easy-reading typesetting, all in a fresh new trim size. Introduce a new generation to these books worth reading!

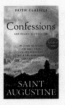

Confessions
by Saint
Augustine

The God of All
Comfort
by Hannah
Whitall Smith

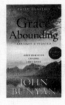

Grace
Abounding
by John Bunyan

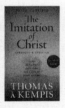

The Imitation
of Christ
by Thomas à
Kempis

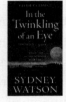

In the
Twinkling of
an Eye
by Sydney
Watson

Quiet Talks
on Prayer
by S.D. Gordon

Each title: Paperback / 4.1875" x 7.5" / 192 pages

Available wherever Christian books are sold.